Prologue

When asked, what I do, my answer regularly is: Business Development, Community Engagement, and building Brand Equity. In other words: Diversity, Equity & Inclusion (DEI) is my schtick and I have dedicated my career to fighting inequality.

DEI initiatives that focus solely on one day of the year will inevitably fail. Simply celebrating International Women's Day on March 8, Pride Day on June 24, or International Men's Day on 19 November won't do.

DEI is a catalyst to raising awareness, mobilizing allies, embedding psychologically safe working practices into business as usual. Enabling DEI to be a thread underlying every business decision, every day of the year. Let's therefore act on the other 364 days.

Warmly,

Christiane.

Prologue

Are we becoming more diverse, or divided? While there is no shortage of good DEI intentions, I believe these efforts are often unfocused, lack measurable goals, fail to address the root causes of inequality and sometimes cause more harm than intended.

This book is meant for leaders seeking to go beyond surface-level performative DEI and effect long-term, systemic change. But this book is also meant for anyone that feels like they don't belong in the world they were born in, myself included. May it serve us as a gateway towards a kinder, more inclusive world.

If diversity is being invited to the party, while inclusion is asked to dance, how can we be sure we aren't "too late to the party"? This book will get you there just in time.

I hope you enjoy reading it, as much as I enjoyed writing it.

Aleks

"Fight for the things that you care about but do it in a way that will lead others to join you."

Ruth Bader Ginsberg

TABLE OF CONTENTS:

THE BROADER CONTEXT

In this section, we address:

- The broad context of D&I comprehensively, addressing common beliefs and myths surrounding the topic
- Hot topics like cultural appropriation and wokeness are explored in-depth, providing readers with a nuanced understanding of the ongoing debate
- A historical perspective on the evolution of D&I, linking it its crucial impact on society today. An outlook into the future with its most recent trends, and – of course – a whole chapter on 'The 'H' in AI".

I. THE EVOLUTION OF DIVERSITY, EQUITY & INCLUSION

Over the past 50 years, DEI has progressed in gender equality, LGBTQ+ rights, and race & ethnicity.

The 1960's and 1970's- women's rights movement focused on workplace and societal gender inequality. The Equal Pay Act of 1963 and the Civil Rights Act of 1964 barred gender-based employment discrimination in the US. Women finally achieved employment equality after decades of agitation and legal fights.

LGBTQ+ rights have also advanced. Before the 1960's, many countries criminalized same-sex partnerships and considered homosexuality a mental disease. The 1990's saw the rise of LGBTQ+ advocacy groups and increased visibility. In 2003, the US Supreme Court overturned state laws criminalizing homosexuality in Lawrence v. Texas, and in 2015, it legalized same-sex marriage nationwide.

African Americans faced widespread discrimination and injustice during the 1950's and 1960's Civil Rights Movement. The Civil Rights Act of 1964 outlawed race, color, religion, sex, and national origin discrimination. Despite legislative protections, racial and ethnic minorities experience inequities in education, employment, and healthcare. The Black Lives Matter movement has revived these problems and started a national discourse about structural racism and social justice in the US.

Diversity, equity, and inclusion have evolved throughout Europe, the UK, Germany, France, Switzerland, Japan, and Asia, too.

Gender equality has improved throughout Europe. Many European countries have legislation promoting gender equality and preventing workplace discrimination, and women have equal pay and opportunities. The 2010 UK Equality Act addresses gender, race, religion, and sexual orientation discrimination.

Europe leads LGBTQ+ rights. Germany recognized same-sex relationships in 1990. Netherlands legalized same-sex marriage first in 2001. Same-sex couples can marry, adopt children, and enjoy legal protection in several European countries, including the UK, Germany, and Switzerland.

Many European countries have regulations to safeguard elderly workers and assure equitable treatment in the workplace. In December 2022 the Swiss Federal Council agreed on the timeline for the implementation of the pension scheme reform that was approved by voters in September. This includes raising the retirement age for women to 65 from 64. By 2028, the retirement age will be for everyone.

Due to colonization and immigration, many European countries have diverse racial and ethnic populations.

Many countries have passed diversity and anti-discrimination laws in recent years to address racial and ethnic imbalances.

Japan has resisted diversity and inclusion for a long time. In recent years, race, ethnicity, gender equality, and LGBTQ+ rights have acquired more importance. Tokyo has become more diverse and inclusive due to the Japanese government's workplace gender equality rules.

The UAE has made strides in diversity and inclusion, particularly in workplace gender equality. Women have had little career progression possibilities and unequal compensation in the UAE, a male-dominated nation. In recent years, the UAE government has promoted gender equality and encouraged more women to work. The UAE has legislation requiring equal pay for equal work and attempts to boost the number of women in leadership roles, particularly STEM women. The UAE promotes cultural sensitivity and treats all employees fairly and respectfully due to its diverse population.

In conclusion, the evolution of diversity, equity, and inclusion has been a complex and ongoing process in the US, Europe, the UK, Germany, France, Switzerland, Japan, the UAE, and Asia. Diversity, fairness, and inclusion have improved over the past 50 years, particularly in gender equality, LGBTQ+ rights, and racial and ethnic equality. Despite recent gains, we must all keep fighting for a more just and equal society.

D&I LEADERS HAVE SEEN THIS PROGRESS

In Western Europe, Diversity & Inclusion could have meant Gender Equality in 2000. Women dominated the early 1900s. The quota was introduced in several European countries, and all efforts were centered on professional development and getting more women to the top. "We don't like a quota, but we like what it does" sums up our stance on this sometimes-heated discussion. We shall discuss gender equality later in the book, but for now it is crucial to emphasize that implementing a quota in Scandinavia initially yielded outstanding results. Women have led groups and inspired other women. This positive discrimination of promoting equally qualified female candidates addressed the substantial underrepresentation of women in leadership.

LGBTQ+ INCLUSION

Two trends emerged ten years ago: "Naming game" first. To promote inclusion, some organizations named the role Inclusion & Diversity (ID). The celebration invites "Diversity" and "Inclusion" to dance. Diversity efforts only succeeded by fostering an inclusive culture. While this goal is great, nine out of 10 companies have yet to figure out how to achieve it. Let alone how to evaluate success. LGBT+ inclusion also topped the agenda. On the other hand, "gender weariness" began to spread. At the same time, we witnessed, and research proved that genuinely modern, innovative, and high-performing firms included the LGBTQ+ community and allies mobilized around this theme. Diversity and inclusion became personal at this point. Diversity & Inclusion grew human when workplaces started talking about sexual orientation (identity came later) and the significant labor and efficiency costs of not being able to "bring your complete self to work." Today, every genuine and effective D&I strategy would include LGBTQ+ Inclusion.

UNFORTUNATE BIAS

Unconscious Bias followed (UB). By this time, Diversity & Inclusion's strategic value was broadly understood, and new roles were established rapidly. Chief Diversity & Inclusion Officer positions were no longer hidden in HR under the Head of Talent. Despite efforts, the change was very gradual. A universal, required instrument was needed. Unconscious Bias trainings began. Thousands of leaders, managers, and employees attended UB trainings and workshops. These were globalized via e-training and often necessary to get traction. What seemed like a compliance exercise, it was supposed to make everyone aware of their own unconscious bias and act on it. We consider time, money, and energy wasted. Instead of well-designed D&I strategies that hold the business accountable, the fix was outsourced and ownership uncertain.

NEW FOCUS ON WAYS OF WORKING

While Gender Equality and LGBTQ+ Inclusion remained significant D&I emphasis topics, it became evident that there was more complexity and that there was something for everyone. Embracing diversity, working with your complete self, and creating an inclusive culture changed how "work" was seen. Companies considered SMART work and trust and individual style. Presenteeism was challenged, and productivity trumped time (in the office). The global COVID-19 pandemic accelerated. Knowledge workers worldwide were obliged to work from home full-time, making Wellbeing and Mental Health the next frontier of D&I.

MIND AND BODY

Pre-pandemic, meditation and yoga lessons were offered along with healthy snacks and fruit bowls. After the pandemic, corporations and executives prioritized employee mental and physical health. Chief Happiness or Wellbeing Officers are common today. The book discusses this and New Ways of Working.

D&I AND THE 'E'

Why is equity a prominent topic in diversity, equity, and inclusion today? Because Diversity, Inclusion, and Equity are nothing without Equity. Equity promotes equitable methods, treatment, and opportunities. It recognizes that oppressive systems have impacted employees differently. Equity redistributes resources and power to mitigate such problems and offers equal opportunity. To develop an enticing organization, we embrace the "E" in Diversity, Equity, and Inclusion.

THE 'T' IN LGBTQ+

The T in LGBTQ+ refers to people whose gender identity differs from the sex they were assigned at birth. Unfortunately, it is true that the T is often forgotten or excluded when discussing LGBTQ rights, which is a phenomenon referred to as "trans erasure", even if they were among the earliest pioneers in the fight for LGBTQ+ rights, throwing the first bricks of resistance at Stonewall. This exclusion happens due to a broader societal tendency to focus on binary gender identities (male and female) rather than non-binary or gender non-conforming identities. But let's not forget, the "T" stands for transgender, not "too difficult to deal with." We are discussing this topic in depth in the chapter of LGBTQ+ Inclusion.

QUICK SUMMARY: THE EVOLUTION OF DIVERSITY, EQUITY & INCLUSION

- The D&I movement started in the 1960's and is not new
- D&I is ever evolving - a journey rather than a destination
- Today D&I mostly extends to: Gender Equality, LGBTQ+ Inclusion, NWOW, Wellbeing & Mental Health, Age Diversity, Socioeconomic Inclusion, Race & Ethnicity and Persons with Disabilities.

II. MYTHS AND COMMON MISTAKES

You might be wondering, why start this book by immediately focusing on the myths and mistakes that happen in the sphere of D&I. Shouldn't we cover the basics first and then the traps you should be watching out for along the way? Indeed, your way of thinking is correct. But these misconceptions about D&I are of utmost importance to be understood from the start and set as the foundations on which this book will uncover the dimensions of inclusion. You will be able to turn the myths into the guiding principles for the work ahead of you. Yes, we do things a bit differently here as you will be able to see while you read this book. You picked it up from the shelf for a reason, right?

All too often, there are a few common myths and misunderstandings that actually can keep you from creating an exemplary diverse and inclusive workplace. Common myths about D&I in the workplace impede leader's ability to address those challenges and meet the goals of an inclusive workplace culture. In the section that follows we are going to uncover and deconstruct some of the most common misconceptions about the D&I work.

TREAT EVERYONE EQUALLY

One of the first and a very common misconception is that to foster diversity and equality in the workplace, you just need to treat everyone equally and somehow magically all will be fixed, assuming that this is what your employees

want and need. While many might be under the assumption that giving everyone the same treatment might be the smart and most fair thing to do, it will only lead to the same unequal outcomes. When you treat everyone equally, it means you provide everyone the same opportunities and resources, ignoring and disregarding the disadvantages that others might have depending on the individual differences.
Imagine you are a coach, and you have a team of ten people. Equality means you will give all of them the same heels. Equity means that you will give each of your players the heels that are their size. Applying this model will get to more equalized outcomes.

If we take this model to the workplace, imagine you have an imbalance of the gender ratio in your IT department (impossible to imagine, I know) and you say to fix this imbalance, you are going to give every candidate while hiring the same treatment and ask them the same questions. The result is still, almost every candidate you end up hiring is someone who identifies as a man. How come, when they were all treated equally? You ask your HR team, and they show you that 90% of the candidates who applied were men, and the justification is that the IT jobs are just attracting more men, there is nothing you can do.

Well, maybe, there still is something you can do. If we try to apply the equity model to this scenario, we are going to investigate the following dimension that recognizes the differences and the obstacles some of the candidates might have faced and have prevented them to applying in the first place. Is the job description using an inclusive language that in not gendered? Did you have a diverse interview panel so the candidates can see someone like them can succeed in your company? Did you upskill your internal candidates in order to help them migrate to a new career? Did you create diverse external talent pools? Did you reach out to universities that have recent diverse graduates? Are you offering flexible benefits? The list goes on and on.

There is a golden rule that is becoming outdated nowadays, but still surfaces the world wide web and can be heard in many meeting rooms and nowadays video calls: “Treat others, the way you want to be treated”. At first it sounds perfectly fair and innocent, but what's the problem with this rule? This rule takes the assumption that you are just like me, and I am like you, and most importantly it is disregarding any differences in our upbringing, life experience and professional journey. The evolved version of this rule has become: “Treat others, the way they want to be treated”. With equity, we are trying to solve the systematic imbalance in our workplaces and our society.

THE DEFICIT MODEL

Perhaps one of the biggest myths surrounding diversity and inclusion (D&I) efforts is that diversity stems from the deficit model, where differences from norms or the dominant culture are seen as an obstacle, or something that needs to be corrected or fixed. With the deficit model, certain groups of people or individuals are perceived as the problem and their life experiences or identities are perceived as weaknesses. Deficit thinking can be traced for hundreds of years back in history, and it has been typically present in dominant classist and racist ideologies.

Consciously or unconsciously, the deficit thinking is applied in many Diversity & Inclusion initiatives: we teach women how to be leaders, we teach members of the LGBTQ+ population to be more confident, we teach POC how to demand a seat at the table, replicating the dominant behavior that got us here in the first place. While such initiatives can yield some results, often it reinforces the separation and segregation of the groups who are being minorized, instead of focusing on how to systematically include them.

For example, when senior leaders are confronted with the facts of inequalities and lack of diversity within their organizations, their immediate excuse is based on the notion "oh, but we only hire based on merit". Whenever a CEO has to announce there are gender goals, quotas or objectives put in place, there is usually a very strong urge to include the concept of meritocracy in the closing statement, as if we are doing something illegal and we need to provide a justification and defend the business case behind D&I. The issue with the so-called merit hiring is that there is an assumption that the merit is reduced to the individual. Whatever success this individual has achieved, it was done all alone, taking out any assistance coming from their upbringing, their identity or background. Until the moment a person from the underrepresented groups is being hired. That is when they are immediately marked as the "diversity hire". So, if you are part of an underrepresented group and you have succeeded, it is only because of the diversity that your identity brings, ergo, anything with not enough merit, has a deficit.

In order to overcome the deficit model behind the D&I effort, as we need to apply a surplus-thinking mindset shift, which recognizes the minoritization of these groups and in turn works on creating new definitions of what are the criteria, norms and expectations that define merit, how does leadership look like and what is the new definition of success. The surplus thinking model recognizes that the individuals from underrepresented groups not only meet the criteria and the conditions needed to be hired/valued/admitted and to be "meritable", but bring additional value that comes from their identities, personal background and their upbringings. These extra values that bring the surplus of qualities are going to become the norms for which every individual has to meet. If we take an example in practical terms, we shouldn't teach women how to be leaders. We should ask women to teach us how to be leaders. This example was most evident during the pandemic, as we realized the countries that had the most successful covid strategies, were countries led by women.

TRAINING IS THE SOLUTION TO EVERYTHING

The fallacy of D&I work being translated into hundreds of training hours on diversity and unconscious bias is hitting the corporate world like a pandemic. When the outcome of an organization's D&I strategy is 90% trainings for their employees, mandatory or optional, it is unfortunately a very clear sign that D&I is a tick the box exercise and the true value of inclusion is far from being seen and recognized. Often titled as the most expensive and least effective training programs, this title belongs to Unconscious Bias trainings. Yet, there are studies that go back to the 1930s which prove the anti-bias training does not reduce the bias or change any behavior. They are also based on the assumption that there is a clear co-relation between bias and discrimination. However, in recent studies it has been proved that changes in unconscious bias does not lead to change in discrimination.

Let there be no mistake, D&I training can be effective and not become a waste of time and money, but not by itself. There are structural norms, processes and policies which must be addressed to support the behavioral change that these trainings are preaching. Moving from unconscious bias to conscious inclusion, these trainings if isolated are not yielding any results. However, when paired with complementary measures, they can help tackle the systematic inequalities of your workplace.

D&I IS PART OF HR

The reason many organizations are now beginning to implement D&I initiatives and strategies is that they finally woke up to the fact that it's one of the key differentiators and the ingrediencies for a successful, innovative and engaged workforce. We will be very straight forward with this one: D&I is a business strategy, not a Human Resources strategy.

There are expectations that if you are already working in HR, you already are very knowledgeable about D&I and the perfect candidate for the role. In the contrary, many D&I leaders in the market have diverse backgrounds and the reality of our world is that HR departments need to also integrate D&I into their practices.

Placing D&I under HR will tie the hands and the scope of the topic to a reduced understanding of what is the impact one can have. D&I is everywhere. Yes, it starts with your people. Then it continues to all the stakeholders in your organization. How you treat your partners, how you treat your suppliers, how diverse is your consumer base and how are you addressing the needs of the underrepresented groups.

Placing D&I under HR will send the signal to every non-HR person in the organization that D&I is simply not their business. HR has been tasked with the job and there is no responsibility for the others. On the contrary, one of the key premises of achieving a greater level of D&I is that everyone, particularly senior business leaders and line managers are responsible for its success and implementation.

Instead of placing D&I under HR, they need to go hand by hand. D&I needs a seat in the boardroom, where the decisions are made.

QUICK SUMMARY: MYTHS & COMMON MISTAKES

- Diversity, Equity, and Inclusion is another HR initiative. D&I expands beyond HR and collaborates with numerous internal and external stakeholders. Anchoring D&I solely within HR might give an excuse to the rest of your organization not to get involved
- D&I is NOT a zero-sum game. The assumption that the inclusion of new people, especially in leadership, leads to the exclusion or expulsion of those who are already there is categorically false. Having a diverse workforce means happier and healthier employees, customers feel more respected, and managers have greater access to the talent and skillset they need for their organizations to thrive
- Pink-washing, rainbow-washing and unconscious bias training work inefficiently.

III. PSYCHOLOGICAL SAFETY

"The belief that one will not be punished or humiliated for speaking up with ideas, questions, concerns, or mistakes, and that the team is safe for interpersonal risk taking." Edmondson, 1999

In today's fast-paced and competitive work environment, it's not uncommon for employees to feel a sense of pressure to constantly perform at their best. "Will I ever be enough if I am not perfect?" "I made a mistake in the excel file formula, probably that's why I won't get a promotion." "My manager asked me for a random 1-1 meeting, will I get punished for calculating the wrong grade for one of my students?" "Insert your own example here whenever you made a mistake, cause we all make them."

While some argue that a certain degree of stress can be motivating, excessive stress can lead people's health and wellbeing down the hill. Striving for a state of psychological safety is crucial, so let's explore together to understand what lies behind this buzzword.

First, let's talk about the basic human need for belonging and connection. Being part of a group, whether it's a family, a friendship circle, or a team at work, is essential for our psychological well-being. But to feel truly connected and invested in a group, we need to feel like we can be ourselves and that we're accepted for who we are.

That's where psychological safety steps in. It gives us the freedom to express ourselves and share our thoughts and ideas without fear of rejection or punishment. When we feel safe in our work environment, we're more likely to open up and form meaningful connections with our colleagues, which leads to better teamwork, productivity, and overall job satisfaction.

Now, let's talk about the brain's threat response system. When we feel like we're in a situation where we're at risk of being judged, rejected, or punished, our brain activates the threat response system, also known as the "fight or flight" response. This response is designed to keep us safe in dangerous situations, but it's not so helpful when it comes to problem-solving and creativity in a work setting. When we're in a state of psychological safety, our brain is in a more relaxed state, which allows us to think more clearly, make better decisions, and come up with innovative ideas. In short, psychological safety is like a warm cozy sweater for our brain, allowing us to feel safe and secure enough to let our guard down and tap into our full potential.

The concept of psychological safety was first introduced by Schein and Bennis in the 1960's, and it was described as a group dynamic that decreases interpersonal risk. They defined it in their 1965 paper "PERSONAL AND ORGANIZATIONAL CHANGE THROUGH GROUP METHODS: THE LABORATORY APPROACH" as something that minimizes "a person's anxiety about being truly accepted and valued." In the years that followed, the concept of psychological safety was brought again to the light in the late 1990s, thanks to the pioneering research of Dr. Amy Edmondson. She coined the term "psychological safety" and conducted a series of studies that showed how it impacted the performance of teams in various industries.

Before that, people have been talking about similar ideas of fostering supportive and non-threatening work environment, which is beneficial for employees and companies. But it was Dr. Edmondson's research that really put the spotlight on psychological safety and made it a hot topic in the world of organizational psychology. Psychological safety quickly became a buzzword in the business world, with companies clamoring to create work environments where employees feel safe to speak up and share their ideas. Google's Project Aristotle was a significant development for the concept of psychological safety, as it provided concrete evidence for what many people already intuitively understood - that the ability to be oneself, share ideas, admit mistakes, respectfully disagree with others, and take risks without fear of failure is a key aspect of human productivity within a team setting. Their research on high performing teams provided evidence that there isn't a single team or employee that does not need a psychologically safe environment to realize their full potential.

But not everyone was convinced of its importance, with some critics dismissing it as yet another fad. However, with the rise of remote working, which highlighted the importance of digital communication, psychological safety has become more important than ever, especially with the concepts of working from home or from anywhere, where trust has been crucial. It has become increasingly clear that creating a culture where employees feel safe to speak up and share their thoughts, concerns and ideas is crucial for the well-being of the employees and the company.

If you are ready to create a workplace where your team members feel comfortable and confident enough to share their ideas, admit their mistakes, and ask for help, keep reading on how to get there.

LEAD BY EXAMPLE

As a leader, it's crucial that you set the tone for the team by being open, vulnerable, and transparent yourself. If you're constantly shooting down new ideas and punishing mistakes, your team members will likely follow suit. But if you are willing to admit when you're wrong and celebrate the successes of your team, they'll feel more comfortable doing the same. So do not shy away from saying "oh, I screwed that up!".

EMBRACE THE AWKWARD

There are no bad ideas. There are no stupid ideas. And it can feel awkward to admit a mistake and be vulnerable in front of your colleagues. Admitting mistakes and asking for help is uncomfortable, but it's an essential part of achieving psychological safety. So, when a team member messes up or needs assistance, don't shy away from the situation. Instead, tackle it head-on and use it as an opportunity to learn and grow together. Teams who fail together, thrive together.

I DON'T KNOW

Normalize to say I don't know. It is far from easy, whether you are a team leader or a team member. There is a lot of shame that comes with this statement and it's a roadblock from getting to psychological safety.

REWARD THE RIGHT BEHAVIOR

Recognize and reward those team members who speak up and take risks, instead of punishing those who make mistakes. And don't be afraid to have fun with it! Maybe you could give a "Risk Taker of the Month" award or something of the sort, which is a playful way to make it clear that you're looking to recognize and appreciate the risk-taking behavior.

It is important to note that in some organizations, culture and management style plays a huge role in how employees feel about failure and making mistakes, that is one of the reasons why creating a culture of psychological safety is important. A culture of psychological safety allows individuals to feel comfortable speaking up and taking risks, knowing they will not be punished for doing so. One mechanism of encouraging the culture of accepting failures is via having some FUN. Yes, this method is quite fun indeed, but in this case, FUN stands for Fu*k Up Nights. The FUN method is based on stories as the core moving force. Stories where your employees are publicly encouraged to share times when they have fu*ked it up and they are going to be celebrated about it. The whole process involves preparations, coaching, selecting carefully the stories and the employees of different levels willing to achieve the ultimate level of vulnerability.

According to the unverified legend, the idea of FUN was initiated when five friends having a night out started wondering why when we meet with others, we always talk about the most obvious success stories of our lives and not about the obvious and hilarious failures because they both exist. Be mindful here, as if your leadership and the organization are not ready, it will turn into quite the opposite effect. Instead of sharing failures, typically senior leaders will wrap the failure story into a humble bragging story where even if there was a major fu*k up, they came out as the heroes of the situation. The aim of a FUN method is to commence a culture of failure, far from being shameful but more as a necessity to create inclusion, creativity and innovation.

As we have seen, psychological safety is the feeling of being able to show up as your authentic self at work, free from the fear of being judged, rejected, or punished. You can speak up, admit mistakes, and ask for help without worrying about the consequences. Remember the sweater we mentioned before? It works the same as a sweater for your body, keeping you comfortable and cozy on a chilly day. The psychological safety sweater for your brains allows you the same - to be comfortable and confident in a work environment. So, let's all strive to create a workplace where we all can feel like we're wrapped up in a warm, fuzzy sweater for the brain, shall we?

QUICK SUMMARY: PSYCHOLOGICAL SAFETY

- Psychological Safety is a precursor to high-performing teams
- Belonging happens when people feel psychologically safe
- Psychological safety is the shared belief that a team is safe for interpersonal risk-taking.

IV. THE 'H' IN AI

: **artificial intelligence (AI),** the ability of a digital computer or computer-controlled robot to perform tasks commonly associated with intelligent beings

: **human (H)**, having the qualities, faults and feelings that people have, as opposed to gods, animals or machines

If we were to ask AI: "What would be the gender of the first female president?", the answer would be "I don't know". Now is the time. And better yesterday. Now is the time to get involved to ensure that AI and AGI (Artificial General Intelligence) create an environment, where we can all bring ourselves.

The AI hysteria that has gripped society recently has caused many to question whether machines will eventually replace humans, rendering us obsolete. This begs the question, why have we allowed ourselves to believe that we are less worthy or equal to AI to even be compared with? Have we become so focused on the technological advancements of AI that we have forgotten the unique qualities that make us human, and instead we believe we are less worthy or equal to a machine that generates clever, human like, biased responses?

The biases present in AI are a stark reminder of the deep-seated prejudices that exist within our society. These biases are not random, nor are they accidental. They are a direct result of the data that is fed into these systems, data that is often skewed towards certain groups and perspectives. The fact that AI can mirror our own biases is not a cause for celebration, but rather a call to action. AI just helps us see even more clearly that our society is riddled with inequalities, and that these inequalities are being reinforced by the technology we create.

Some may argue that the biases present in AI are simply a reflection of the biases that exist within the human brain and that's how humans are. This is a dangerous line of thinking, one that absolves us of responsibility for creating a better future. We cannot simply throw up our hands and say, "that's just the way things are." Ethical AI is on the rise, ensuring that the data it uses represents a diverse range of perspectives and the outputs it creates are inclusive and promote equality and exposing the dark side of AI. There can be a future where technology is a force for good, rather than a reminder of our own prejudices.

We can see a well-developed AI like an adult cis white straight man. He grew up picking up lots of useful and harmful behaviors and biases from society, privileged, mansplaining and always providing an output, (even if the AI has no data on the topic). Now it's time to unlearn a thing or two. And between the two species, we have a small feeling that it might be a bit easier to teach an AI machine how to unlearn things. Call us naïve, perhaps the timing of the "rise of the machines" is exactly what the doctor ordered. Maybe it is time for us to be reminded that we are more than our social media feeds, our purchasing history, beauty filters and Outlook emails. And that we are. The deep complexity of the humankind, our life experiences, energies, diverse backgrounds and unpredictable spontaneous emotions is the iceberg, and what AI mimics we are, is just the tip that is visible on the surface.

The human nature is fluid. For AI to function, it has to be taught and trained and relies on data as the inputs to create a human like output. But, do we even know ourselves, to teach someone, or something, how to be human? AI is a work in progress and we, as human beings, are a work in progress as well. Sometimes it seems that we are not allowing AI to make any mistakes, be biased and then learn from its mistakes, or with other words, we are not allowing AI to act like...a human?

That just might be it, the key to this puzzle. We are those always evolving, ever fluid, empathic, intellectual, unique, irrational, highly conflicting human beings, and good luck to any AI trying to catch up with that.

We close with a quote that we trust it will navigate us through the next steps:

"AI should be a mirror of the best of who we are, not the worst. We must infuse our systems with empathy, compassion, and understanding, to create technologies that truly enrich and elevate the human experience."

Lex Fridman

QUICK SUMMARY: THE ‘H’ in AI

- The moment is now to act upon making sure that there is enough ‘H’ in AI
- There is a real danger of AI bias. AI bias is the underlying prejudice in data that’s used to create AI algorithms, which can ultimately result in discrimination and other social consequences
- Another reason why AI might be discriminatory is quite obvious: The lack of diversity in the sector.

V. NWOW - THE FUTURE OF WORK

While we are observing strong shifts in the manufacturing environment as well, our focus here is on work in the context of a *knowledge worker* defined as a person, whose job involves handling or using information. The term *knowledge worker* was first coined by Peter Drucker in his book *The Landmarks of Tomorrow (1959*). Drucker defined knowledge workers as high-level workers who apply theoretical and analytical knowledge, acquired through formal training, to develop products and services. In short: their capital is knowledge. He noted that knowledge workers would be the most valuable assets of a 21st-century organization because of their high-level productivity and creativity.

Statistical information confirms that the share of manual workers in the labor force has been decreasing, while the share of white-collar jobs has been on the rise. According to Gartner, there are currently a staggering **one billion** knowledge workers across the globe, whose jobs specifically require them to combine action with level of domain expertise - their knowledge - to generate value and make critical decisions. Examples include programmers, physicians, pharmacists, journalists, architects, engineers, scientists, design thinkers, public accountants, lawyers, editors and academics, whose job is 'to think for a living'.

Knowledge workers have a higher job-mobility, they can work in different time zones, at home, in airport lounges, co-working spaces and coffee-shops.

Now, why was it ever a good idea, to have knowledge workers a) commute to an office, b) working from 9-to-5 for c) five days a week? As we will see later, dramatic shifts are here to stay impacting a)-c).

To better understand the future, we need to look at the evolution of work and the broader context of history.

THE HISTORY OF WORK

The **50's** were a watershed moment in history. Women had surged into the workforce during World War II, accounting for 32% of the US workforce by 1950. In the 1950's, more African Americans worked in offices, and African American men narrowed the income gap between African American men and white men by about a third. The factory floor inspired office layouts, with rows and rows of desks crammed tightly together. Meanwhile, executives enjoyed private corner offices with large windows to ensure that everyone was working hard. Manual typewriters and adding machines were among the first pieces of technology to enter the workplace, but they had the unfortunate side effect of making offices extremely noisy.

1960's - What you might have seen on the hit show Mad Men isn't all that dissimilar to office life in the 1960's. In the office, drinking and smoking were common, and the 'three-martini lunch' was born. 'Action Office 2' was created. Former art professor Robert Probst and Herman Miller launched the Action Office 2 in 1968, a single, easy-to-assemble unit with vertical partitions to reduce distraction. You've probably heard of the cubicle. International Business Machines (IBM) emerged as the leading provider of workplace technology. It introduced an electric typewriter, which increased typists' speed and productivity, as well as a computer system for business customers. IBM was fulfilling 1000 orders per month within two years.

1970's - The revolutionary 1960's influenced people's attitudes for the next decade. They began to look away from government and toward the private sector for economic solutions. Personal liberation and rebellion became the Western World's hallmarks of the 1970's: long hair, outrageous clothing, and strong individualism. Businesses still had dress codes, but they were enforced to varying degrees. Many countries' economies collapsed in 1975, resulting in job insecurity for the first time in decades. When the term "sexual harassment in the workplace" was coined in the United States in 1974, it exploded onto the scene. The fax machine was a huge success, and IBM introduced the first high-speed laser printer in 1967. Floppy disks, which could hold 1.44 megabytes of data, became commercially available in 1971.

1980's - Despite having two recessions in three years and surviving a one-day stock market crash (Black Monday - a 22.6% drop in a single day), the 1980's ended with 19 million more jobs. The beginning of the 9-to-5. People began to discuss and advocate for work-life balance, and wellness programs became commonplace in the workplace. The importance of corporate culture was emphasized. It was critical that the company had a culture, that it was defined, and that every employee was aware of it. A famous example and front-runner we saw in General Electric (GE) with their four core values: EDGE, ENERGY, EXECUTION, and EXCELLENCE. In the 90's each GE employee around the globe would have been able to quote these as the 4 E's. Workplace technology was becoming increasingly important, with personal computers appearing on nearly every desk. The Macintosh was introduced in 1984, the first dotcom address was registered in 1985, and the World Wide Web (www) went live for the first time in 1989.

1990's - Employees began to question the value of long-term company loyalty and began prioritizing their own needs and interests over those of their employers. 'Office Space,' which debuted in 1999, satirized the mundane, everyday work of office workers and their incompetent, overbearing bosses. Companies that failed to consider quality-of-life issues when implementing total quality management (Six Sigma), re-engineering, or any other of the competitiveness-enhancing, productivity-improving schemes that were popular at the time may gain little more than a view of their best people leaving for friendlier premises. 'Casual Friday' arrived on the scene, where employees would forego their typical suits and dresses on the last day of the workweek in favor of jeans, chinos, and sneakers. Later in the decade, the dot-com industry grew rapidly. Yahoo and Netscape were among the major technology IPOs. The birth of Amazon and eBay signaled the beginning of a new era in e-commerce. Cellphones, the first email, and Personal Digital Assistants were among the leading technologies of the time (PDAs).

Despite the dotcom bust, widespread use of technology in the workplace began to affect low-wage, low-education jobs in the **2000s**. Just as technology reduced the number of factory floor jobs, it also reduced the number of administrative assistants, bank tellers, and retail workers. Significant changes in the workplace were being driven by shifting economic landscapes. Jobs requiring higher-level social or analytical skills, or both, were becoming more common. Physical or manual skills, which were once as valuable as social or analytical skills, were rapidly fading in importance. Not surprisingly, employment was increasing faster in jobs that required more preparation, whether through education, experience, or other forms of training. Our knowledge worker from above assumed command. The proportion of American women over the age of 16 in the labor force peaked in April 2000, at 60%. (It has never been higher, even today.) The cubicle is doomed. Whatever allure the cubicle had in the 1960's had faded by the new millennium. The early 2000's saw the rise of the open-floor office plans and more became 'telecommuting'. So much of the technology we use today was developed or introduced in the 2000s: Skype in 2003, Google (IPO in 2004), Gmail in 2004, Facebook in 2004, Twitter in 2006, and the iPhone in 2007.

2010's - The global economy slowly but steadily recovered from the 2008 recession and financial crisis, the worst since the Great Depression. Globalization and the loss of many retail jobs during the recession caused the Western economy to shift from manufacturing to services, specifically healthcare, financial services, and social assistance. The technology sector has grown to be a significant global economic component. From 2016 to 2026, employment in technology and information technology is expected to grow 13 percent, faster than the average for all occupations. The workforce is more diverse than it has ever been. In many offices, representatives from four generations are working together: Baby Boomers, Generation X, Generation Y and Millennials. Ethnic diversity has also reached an all-time high in the United States, the United Kingdom, and other parts of Continental Europe. Artificial Intelligence (AI), which connects everything we do in business and governs daily life, is one of the decade's leading technologies and innovations. Popular workplace productivity tools include Slack, Microsoft Teams, and Google Docs. Mobile apps are breaking into the business world. Workers can store and access massive amounts of data online thanks to the Cloud.

2020 - So, what now? Looking at the timeline above, it's safe to say that work and the workplace have seen continuous improvement. Never have we seen such a diverse workforce, the importance of a healthy work environment and culture, and the shared responsibility of leadership and employees to create an inclusive, modern, and tech-savvy workplace. Work will become increasingly distributed, asynchronous, and location-independent. AI and automation are making this shift as significant as mechanization in previous generations of agriculture and manufacturing. While some jobs will be lost and many new ones created, almost everything will change. The COVID-19 crisis accelerated existing trends and forced organizations to rethink many aspects of their operations. The 9-to-5 workday is an industrial revolution relic. The post-pandemic digital age is reorienting our world for work that can be done at any time and from any location. Stephane Kasriel, CEO of Upwork, stated in a 2017 article for the World Economic Forum (WEF) that most of the US workforce will be freelance by 2027.

THE ROLE OF THE OFFICE

With work having shifted to anywhere, the role of the (traditional) office is under scrutiny. The most forward-looking solution we could find is that of *Salesforce*. 'Forget the Office – *Salesforce* is making a Wellness Retreat their Headquarter' quotes the Wall Street Journal (WSJ) on 10 February 2022. Employees, Leaders and Associates will come to 'the office' to collaborate, bond, communicate, brainstorm and co-create. In addition, they will want to invest in their wellbeing, mental health and... have some fun together. Coming together on a quarterly basis for quality time with colleagues is replacing the daily commute to the office. And let's not be fooled by what seemingly looks like a luxury spent. Reducing office space in high-cost locations easily offsets the cost of entering a multi-year-lease of a Wellness Retreat. The sense of belonging will be cultivated, and this is such a smart way to engage with your employees.

We recommend that employers, whether a large multinational player or a Small-Medium-Enterprise (SME), repurpose their offices in a way that embraces collaboration and creates an incentive for employees to come to the office in the first place.

Equally, smart organizations wanting to stay attractive and relevant will consider financial and non-financial support for the set-up of their employee's home office. We have seen a lot of progress rethinking the office, while forgetting about the working hours employees are dedicating by working from home or elsewhere. This will include state-of-the-art technology and IT-equipment and / or a lump sum payment for employees to set up their home office in a way that supports their wellbeing and create a productive environment.

MEETING RESET

In early January 2023, Shopify announced a new policy for the calendar: It's dropping meetings for employees in the new year. With immediate effect, all recurring meetings with more than two people are being removed from internal calendars, with a two-week period instituted before employees are allowed to add anything back. They will also ban meetings on Wednesdays, and limit large meetings to a strict window on Thursdays. Shopify isn't the first company to try a calendar blow-up and we already see others following this trend.

As for virtual meetings, we recommend investing into modern video-call technology that allows an inclusive participation of all. Gone are the days, when dialing into a conference call from home meant that one couldn't understand a word that was said, let alone being part of the conversation. Leaders run a successful meeting, when all meetings are set remote as default and are run equally seamless, wherever you are.

WORKING FROM 9-TO-5 IS OVER

Work has shifted from 9-to-5 to **whenever**. This asynchronous working allows for the appreciation of individual 'body clocks' or circadian rhythms as well as working across time zones. Not everyone is an early riser, and a night owl may be ideal for working from Australia and collaborating with European clients.

Employees can set their own work hours with asynchronous work, which does not require them to be online and responsive at the same time every day. Asynchronous work is work that can be completed at a convenient time within a set period of time. As a result, it is not reliant on real-time communication and collaboration. Instead, it is dependent on clear goals, standards, and team commitment.

The most important distinction between synchronous and asynchronous work is how much time employees are expected to be online, responsive, and available at work. Work and communication are separated by asynchronous work.

Goals and outcomes have taken the place of measuring pure time and activity. Asynchronous managers prioritize setting clear goals and expectations, whereas synchronous work managers frequently prioritize controlling and measuring employees' time at work and daily activity.

Aside from this management style, another requirement for successful asynchronous work is that teams rely on defined workflows and processes to progress rather than constant back-and-forth communication and one-on-one conversations. To be efficient and productive, the right technology in the form of chat tools like Slack is essential. Asynchronous work prefers documentation and transparency to time-consuming communication and silos. It encourages a more structured flow of communication by relying on a single source of truth to reduce ambiguity and confusion in workplace matters. Hallelujah! This gets everyone on the same page and helps the work move forward without hiccups.

Let us conclude this section on asynchronous work with a discovery that blew our minds when we looked deeper into this at the start of the pandemic: what is the single most important skill required? What is the first thing a recruiter looks for when evaluating candidates for their ability to work from anywhere? English writing abilities! When you think about it, it makes perfect sense. With written communication becoming more prevalent, and English arguably being the global business language, you will want to invest in or hire for written English skills.

U-WORK BY UNILIVER

A special shout-out - yet again - goes to Unilever. An organization that has been pioneering and role modeling Diversity & Inclusion in the workplace for decades. Addressing the future of work and the increased demand for more flexibility, Unilever has introduced U-Work in 2021. U-work gives employees the freedom and flexibility associated with contract roles with the security and benefits typically linked to permanent roles. We would call this: Bringing the gig-economy inside your organization. People at Unilever in U-Work don't have a fixed role. They work on varying assignments, and between assignments are free to do other things that are important to them. They get a monthly retainer and a specially designed suite of benefits whether they're working on an assignment or not. They can design work patterns that suit them - anything from a few days a week for a few months, to short, concentrated bursts of full-time with breaks in-between. And they get paid for each assignment when they're working.

THE FOUR-DAY WEEK IS HERE!

... and it's not going away anytime soon. The four-day workweek was an "overwhelming success" in Iceland, according to the BBC on July 5, 2021. Between 2015 and 2019, Iceland conducted trials in which workers were paid the same amount for working fewer hours. According to the researchers, productivity in most workplaces remained stable or improved.

Several trials are now underway around the world, including those with Microsoft in Japan, Unilever in New Zealand, Spain, Belgium, the United States, Canada, Australia, Ireland, and, most recently, the United Kingdom in 2022.

The UK pilot has been equally successful to date and has continued until December 31, 2022. On September 22, 2022, the New York Times reports that the UK's 4-day workweek causes no productivity loss. Over 70 companies in the United Kingdom are participating in a six-month experiment in which their employees receive a paid day off each week. In simple terms, participating workplaces follow the 100-80-100-rule, which we like because it is simple and compelling: workers will continue to receive 100% of their salary while working time is reduced to 80%, with the goal of maintaining 100% productivity. 4 Day Week Global is coordinating the pilot in collaboration with the UK Think Tank Autonomy, the 4 Day Week UK Campaign, Boston College, and Oxford University.

If you and your organization are considering conducting a 4-day-week experiment, the following resources may be helpful:

- Create and run workshops within your organization based on other successful examples and those who have successfully implemented a 4-day week. Webinars on online resources to assist with common challenges, pitfalls, and how to deal with misconceptions should be included.

- Seek out mentors from other organizations and look for a match in experience that best suits your organization's unique needs.

- Begin networking with organizations that have successfully transitioned to a 4-day workweek or with organizations that specialize in this field.

- Start by having a team of experts within or outside your organization conduct a Wellbeing & Productivity assessment to define what success looks like for you. Creating Wellbeing and Productivity metrics for your organization and anonymously monitoring them throughout the trial.

We believe that when the chapter for this decade is written, the 4-day workweek will be the new global work standard in the 2020s. Join the movement and begin your experimentation right away!

QUICK SUMMARY: NWOW - THE FUTURE OF WORK

- The future of works describes changes in how work will get done over the next decade, influenced by technological, generational, and societal shifts
- Work will increasingly be a fluid-concept and the standard 9-to-5 working week will be rare, while the divisions between home and work further blur and non-financial rewards are given in trade-off for less money
- The inclusive workplace in high demand: organizations' shift their attention to racial injustice and equity, including real commitments and investments in doing better.

VI. #METOO, WOKE, CANCEL CULTURE AND CULTURAL APPROPRIATION

The most serious threat to progress in Diversity, Equity, and Inclusion is here: #MeToo, the so-called cancel culture, accusations of cultural appropriation, and the entire unhealthy debate over wokeness. The pendulum isn't just swinging; it's swinging in unpredictable directions, and we're facing what we call an UBER-correction. We fear that this political and cultural movement might turn off those who are otherwise sympathetic to the cause of D&I. Instead, we invite everyone to embrace and live with ambiguity, and to approach the morality cause with Love and Kindness.

#METOO

#MeToo is a social movement against sexual abuse, sexual harassment, and rape culture in which people share their sexual abuse or sexual harassment experiences. The goal of "Me Too," as it was first expressed in 2006, was to empower sexually assaulted people (particularly young and vulnerable women) through empathy, solidarity, and strength in numbers. This was achieved by visibly demonstrating how many people have experienced sexual assault and harassment in the workplace and on university campuses.

After millions of people began using the phrase #MeToo in this manner, the expression spread to dozens of other languages. With the expansion, the scope has become somewhat broader, and it is now referred to as an international movement for justice for marginalized people, with the hashtag #MeToo going viral ever since.

CANCEL CULTURE

The Merriam-Webster dictionary defines *cancel culture* as 'the practice or tendency of engaging in mass cancellation as a way of expressing disapproval and exerting social pressure'. The term "cancel culture" was first used in 2016. The 'cancel culture' (the cancellation of the past culture) is a movement specifically in the United States that has had reached Europe. *Le Monde* titles in January 2023 'Intellectuals in France call out the rise of cancel culture'. We have seen similar headlines from *Repubblica* in Italy and the *Neue Zürcher Zeitung* in Switzerland. The list of individuals and brands that have been cancelled to date is long.

CULTURAL APPROPRIATION

When members of a majority group adopt cultural elements of a minority group in an exploitative, disrespectful, or stereotypical manner, this is referred to as cultural appropriation.

Cultural appropriation occurs when a member of a majority group profits financially or socially from the culture of a minority group. Madonna released the music video for her song "Vogue" in 1990, which featured the voguing dance, pioneered by the community of African American and Latinx LBGTQ+ creatives who used balls and voguing to create their own universe of self-expression, separate from the society from which they were marginalized. Even though Madonna included performers from the community in the video, ostensibly to honor the dance's origins, she was the one who benefited when "Vogue" went double platinum in the United States. By some, Madonna's use of voguing was considered cultural appropriation and not appreciation, because she gained financial and cultural capital from it in a way that its creators did not, even if she took all the right steps in doing so.

A more recent example occurred in Switzerland:

Lauwarm, a Swiss reggae band, performed at Bern's Brasserie Lorraine on July 18, 2022. The band performs Jamaican music, sings in Swiss dialect, and wears dreadlocks and African ethnic clothing. This attire irritated some customers, with "several people" expressing "discomfort with the situation," according to the restaurant's Facebook page, where the incident was made public on July 25, 2022, claiming this would constitute cultural appropriation. The restaurant decided to cancel the concert after speaking with the band. The restaurant apologized to "everyone for whom the concert had caused bad feelings". The following day it issued a statement specifying "that members of the band or white people are not automatically racists". In April 2023 a dance ensemble of German pensioners wasn't allowed to wear sombreros at the Federal Garden Show.

Another twisted example is that of Meg Smaker, an American documentary filmmaker, editor, and producer.

Sundance liked her documentary on terrorism, until Muslim critics didn't, according to the New York Times on September 25, 2022. The film festival selected Meg Smaker's "Jihad Rehab" for its 2022 lineup, but later apologized for her race and approach. The attacks would come from the left, not the right, as had been predicted. Ms. Smaker was accused of Islamophobia and American propaganda by Arab and Muslim filmmakers and their white supporters. Some questioned her eligibility because she was a white woman telling the story of Arab men. Sundance executives changed their minds and apologized. The documentary directed by Meg Smaker has been canceled. Meg has only able to screen her film in (very) select movie theaters both inside and outside of the United States in 2022 and thanks to a highly successful crowdfunding campaign she's been able to bring the movie to theaters herself in 2023.

WOKENESS

What a strange word that has become so familiar that it is now part of our common language. The Cambridge Dictionary defines wokeness as "a state of being aware, especially of social problems such as racism and inequality." In his opinion piece titled 'The War on Wakefulness,' Charles M. Blow writes in the New York Times on November 10, 2021. „Wakefulness has been described in the most oblique terms imaginable, from ideology to religion to cult. It has become so derided and adulterated that young people who would have been considered woke five years ago no longer use the term."

Without even delving into the debate and debacle on all of the above, our concern here is the impact on Diversity, Equity, and Inclusion and how the discourse is being captured.

A WAY FORWARD

We found solace in the Law. Consider the dynamic of intent vs. impact as a constructive way out of this mess. In general, intent refers to the mental goal behind an action, and as such, the concept of intent is frequently the focal point in law. In many recent cases of cancel culture or cultural appropriation, the concept of intent has been abandoned in favor of measuring only the perceived impact. Anyone, heightened by the social media frenzy, could claim that an action or statement marginalized, discriminated against, or exploited them. However, we cannot ignore the concept of intent altogether. Only when both, the marginalizing, exploiting, or discriminating intent **and** the respective impact exist, is there a case to cancel or to rightfully claim cultural appropriation. In these cases, we should absolutely do so! The debate over cancel culture began as a search for accountability, but it may end up being about encouraging empathy.

The above, taken to its logical conclusion, only leads to what we can best describe as an Italian dinner table: Everyone is yelling at each other, and no one is paying attention. (Warning: cultural appropriation). Let's calm down and regain our composure. There is simply too much at stake. Cancel culture and its most vicious proponents thrive on attention, so bringing it up in every instance –

especially in a negative light – only exacerbates the problem and draws it back into the spotlight. While homophobia, racism, sexism, ableism, and transphobia all exist at different levels of society, making fun of them only exacerbates already bad situations. The world is far more nuanced, interconnected, and beautiful than stereotype-based behavior suggests, and it's unfortunate that such behavior exists. Madonna and Meg Smaker, on the other hand, are role models, who, with the best of intentions and years of professional flesh and blood, should be allowed to create art that inspires and makes us think.

Working in D&I means walking this fine line every day: knowing when to speak up and to challenge the status quo, and when to shut the f* * * up.

QUICK SUMMARY: #METOO, WOKE, CANCEL CULTURE & CULTURAL APPROPRIATION

- What started with #Metoo, led to the birth of cancel culture, wokeness and cultural appropriation
- These can have a chilling effect on public discourse, might be unproductive, don't bring real social change, can cause intolerance and amount to cyberbullying
- Might be hampering your Diversity, Equity, and Inclusion plans.

VII. THE 'S' IN ESG

Is 'green washing' the new 'pink washing' and how are the two connected?

As D&I leaders, we have a bit of a déjà vu when we are confronted by the news about organizations and how they are accused of green washing. But let's start from the top:

ESG stands for **E**nvironmental, **S**ocial, and **G**overnance. Investors are increasingly applying these non-financial factors as part of their analysis process to identify material risks and growth opportunities. ESG takes the holistic view that sustainability extends beyond just environmental issues. While the term ESG is often used in the context of investing, stakeholders include not just the investment community but also customers, suppliers, and employees, all of whom are increasingly interested in how sustainable an organization's operations are.

The 'S', the social pillar, refers to an organization's relationships with stakeholders. Examples of factors that a company may be measured against include Human Capital Management and D&I metrics like fair wages, employee engagement and inclusion. A hallmark of ESG is how social impact expectations have extended outside the walls of the company and to supply chain partners, particularly those in developing economies where environmental and labor standards may be less robust.

With this, diversity & inclusion considerations are high on the ESG agenda, as business strive to reflect their customers and communities. Hence, in the context of ESG, it is often referred to the 'S' in ESG.

#5 of the United Nations Sustainable Development Goals (SDG 5)

One very specific example is the inclusion under #5 of the Sustainable Development Goals by the UN and reads as follows: "Gender Equality is not only a fundamental human right, but a necessary foundation for a peaceful, prosperous and sustainable world.". As a result, SDG #5 is aimed to "achieve gender quality and empower all women and girls".

The specific targets under this goal are:

- 5.1 End all forms of discrimination against all women and girls everywhere
- 5.2 Eliminate all forms of violence against all women and girls in the public and private spheres, including trafficking and sexual and other types of exploitation
- 5.3 Eliminate all harmful practices, such as child, early and forced marriage and female genital mutilation
- 5.4 Recognize and value unpaid care and domestic work through the provision of public services, infrastructure and social protection policies and the promotion of shared

responsibility within the household and the family as nationally appropriate

- 5.5 Ensure women's full and effective participation and equal opportunities for leadership at all levels of decision-making in political, economic and public life
- 5.6 Ensure universal access to sexual and reproductive health and reproductive rights as agreed in accordance with the Programme of Action of the International Conference on Population and Development and the Beijing Platform for Action and the outcome documents of their review conferences.
- 5.A Undertake reforms to give women equal rights to economic resources, as well as access to ownership and control over land and other forms of property, financial services, inheritance and natural resources, in accordance with national laws.
- 5.B Enhance the use of enabling technology, in particular information and communications technology, to promote the empowerment of women.
- 5.C Adopt and strengthen sound policies and enforceable legislation for the promotion of gender equality and the empowerment of all women and girls at all levels.

If we were to sum it up visually in a Venn Diagram, we would see the circle for Diversity & Inclusion on the left and ESG on the right with an overlapping circle in the middle showing the commonality. Within organizations this leads to a very close cooperation between the D&I and Corporate Sustainability Team. Both are working together towards the common goals and are equally held accountable by employees and the leadership alike, to have a sound understanding of the whole spectrum.

With the demand for greater transparency around companies' strategy and progress on ESG, many struggle with how to measure the topics within the 'S' pillar. These topics are broad, ranging from human capital development to community relations to social opportunities, such as access to finance and health care, and how to measure progress and impact aren't always tangible. Diversity & Inclusion, an increasingly important component of the 'S' in ESG, is no different. And while many CEOs are committed to D&I and its impact on both internal company values and long-term value creation, companies may face another layer of complexity as their leaders learn more about employee perceptions of corporate culture and establish aspirational goals.

To overcome some common barriers to ESG, and specifically D&I reporting, Executives can embrace three leading practices: build an authentic story, engage the right leaders and take a data driven approach.

A lot can and should be learned from the backlash of 'pink washing' to avoid falling into the trap of 'green washing'.

How so? When we talk about 'pink washing', we mean the practice of a company presenting itself as gay-friendly and progressive to downplay or brush over its negative behavior. Before turning your company logo into a rainbow-colored one on social media, it is a must to have your house in order first. Next to 'pink washing', we have come across 'rainbow washing' and, why not take it all, 'diversity washing'. It all leads to the same conclusion, Diversity & Inclusion have become key buzzwords in the corporate world, leading to a very real risk that companies are leveraging these terms for their own brand image and monetary gains, instead of focusing on making a real change. As part of the now required ESG reporting, this risk will be amplified.

- Strategy: It starts with having a clearly outlined D&I action plan, backed with financial commitment.

- Data: Measure your progress. It's great to have several initiatives, but these need to be linked to key KPIs to show real impact.

- Governance: The ultimate way to prevent all talk and no action is by holding people accountable. Clear roles & responsibilities in place for the ERGs, the leadership, employees, D&I, Human Resources and the Global Diversity Advisory Council as oversight.

- Leadership: When it comes to behavior and culture, sustainability is key. Walking the talk not only one, but also on *the other 364 days* of the year.

- Systems: The last pillar focuses on inclusive policies, processes, and practices. From both an internal and an external lens. It is critical to open up and undergo an external assessment of all of the above.

This is where *The Inclusion Foundation™* and its certificate overlaps with organizations like B Corp (www.bcorporation.net). There is a strong relationship between ESG and Diversity & Inclusion for long-term sustainability. It is therefore irresponsible to stop investing in Diversity & Inclusion during tough times. Quite the opposite, organizational investments that are driven by D&I priorities can have a positive impact on the bottom line.

QUICK SUMMARY: THE “S” IN ESG

- The “S” in ESG or: how to invest in your people
- The social component of ESG covers all the ways companies interact with their employees and communities in which they operate
- How corporations measure their social impact can greatly influence how they address the wellbeing of their employees, communities, and other stakeholders.

VIII. THE INCLUSION FOUNDATION™

For us, advocating for fairness, equity, Diversity & Inclusion in the workplace has been and will be a matter of the heart and the mind. We saw first-hand and times and times again the incredible positive change, once an organization, its leadership and employees got on board. D&I is a team-sport and we remain incredibly grateful for the CEOs, who put their trust and confidence in us and the process. We are equally in debt to every single colleague and employee, who got inspired and continues to carry the flame to ignite further positive change.

Today, the Diversity & Inclusion industry is a billion-dollar business. McKinsey & Company published on 13 January 2023 that "In 2020, the global market for D&I – that is, dollars spent by companies on D&I-related efforts – was estimated at USD 7.5billion and is projected to more than double to USD 15.4billion by 2026".

Very smart and successful D&I leaders are managing large teams and a substantial budget. Small-to-medium-sized companies, NGOs, governmental organizations and academia are incredibly impressive in how they embrace D&I, shape its future and move the agenda along.

'MEETING AN UNMET NEED'

Lending this approach from the pharmaceutical industry. "Unmet healthcare needs are determined as the difference between the services judged necessary and the services actually received" writes the National Institute of Health (NIH). Unmet needs or demands are not satisfied. Over the years, we got increasingly 'not satisfied' with the way, companies were assessed, benchmarked, reviewed or labelled in the space of D&I. Either the scope was too narrow, i.e., only looking at Equal Pay. Or too wide, for example as a small part of the annual employee engagement survey. Other benchmarks are industry indexes measuring only Gender Equality and its impact on the equity market. Plus, there are several 'labels', mainly in the space of LGBTQ+ Inclusion. While others reflect the D&I commitment by signing a Charta.

Don't get us wrong, we worked with all the above and couldn't have done our job without them. We highly respect the people involved and the outcome, data and/or impact they provide. These tools are relevant and indispensable to quality D&I progress. But still, something was missing, and we got increasingly 'not satisfied'. What was lacking was an approach that brings it all together.

THE INCLUSION FOUNDATION™

"What is needed, is a) a neutral and qualified third-party advisor with b) sound and practical D&I expertise, looking at c) all relevant dimensions of D&I, adjusted to d) modern times, where e) AI is used to measure inclusion with a f) measurable outcome"

This is the problem statement we took to the smartest brains in D&I and, as a result, we came up with a product and decided to found '*The Inclusion Foundation™*'

www.theinclusionfoundation.com. We will put our combined 50+ years' experience to work by providing the next level D&I independent certification, across the seven dimensions of D&I discussed in this book. Where smart AI will enable us to effectively measure the inclusion and potential exclusion within organizations. Selected ones will be able to demonstrate their genuine commitment to D&I via the certification by the Inclusion Foundation™.

QUICK SUMMARY: THE INCLUSION FOUNDATION ™

- An independent, third party verified company based in Switzerland that certifies organizations around the world in Diversity, Equity, and Inclusion
- The assessment spans over seven key dimensions of D&I: Gender Balance, LGBTQ+ Inclusion, Race & Ethnicity, Persons with Disabilities, Wellbeing & Mental Health, NWOW the future of work and Age Diversity
- A smart approach using AI to measure Inclusion (ONA) is embedded.

IX. INTERSECTIONALITY

: the complex, cumulative process by which the effects of multiple forms of discrimination (such as ageism, racism, sexism, and classism) combine, overlap, or intersect, particularly in the experiences of marginalized individuals or groups. Intersectionality has grown in importance in the field of diversity and inclusion, particularly in the United States and Europe. Intersectionality is a concept that recognizes the interconnected nature of various forms of discrimination and how they overlap and compound to create unique marginalization and discrimination experiences.

Intersectionality was coined by critical race scholar Kimberle Crenshaw in the late 1980's and has since been used to analyze and address the ways in which multiple forms of discrimination intersect. Intersectionality, for example, can assist organizations in understanding how gender, age, and socioeconomic diversity overlap and compound. A woman who is also older may face discrimination that is different from that experienced by a younger woman or older man. Similarly, a person who is a member of a racial minority and also low income may face discrimination that is distinct from that experienced by a member of the same racial minority who is not low income.

THE UNITED STATES, INTERSECTIONALITY

Let's start with the most recent data on what Intersectionality means in real numbers in the United States:

McKinsey's Women in the Workplace report is in its eighth year (released 18, October 2022). This effort, conducted in collaboration with LeanIn.Org, is the largest study of women in corporate America. This year, they gathered data from 333 participating organizations employing over 12 million people, surveyed over 40,000 employees, and interviewed women of diverse identities – including women of color, LGBTQ+ women, and women with disabilities – to gain an intersectional view of biases and barriers.

Their research revealed that, in the midst of the "Great Breakup," women in the United States are demanding more from their jobs, and they are leaving in unprecedented numbers to get it. Women leaders are changing jobs at an unprecedented rate – and at a higher rate than men in leadership. This could have serious consequences for businesses. Women are already underrepresented in positions of leadership. Because of the "broken rung" at the first step up to management, fewer women have risen through the ranks for years. Companies are now struggling to retain the few female executives they have. All of these dynamics are exacerbated for women of color.

The reasons why female executives are leaving their companies are instructive. Women leaders are just as ambitious as men, but in many companies, they face roadblocks that indicate it will be more difficult to advance. They are more likely to encounter belittling microaggressions, such as having their judgment called into question or being mistaken for someone younger. They are doing more to promote employee well-being and inclusion, but this important work is spreading them thin and going mostly unnoticed. Finally, it is becoming increasingly important for female leaders to work for companies that value flexibility, employee well-being, and diversity, equity, and inclusion.

Many women face discrimination not only because of their gender, but also because of their race, sexual orientation, disability, or other aspects of their identity – and the sum of the whole is much greater than the individual parts. As a result, these women frequently face more microaggressions and face greater barriers to advancement. Notably, despite receiving less support, women of color are more ambitious: according to McKinsey, 41 percent of women of color want to be top executives, compared to 27 percent of White women. Companies and coworkers must be aware of these dynamics in order to more effectively promote equity and inclusion for all women. Although no study can fully capture the experiences of women with historically marginalized identities, the findings this year point to these distinct experiences:

Latinas and Black women are less likely than women of other races and ethnicities to say their boss encourages their professional development. They also have less psychological safety – for example, less than half of Latinas and Black women say mistakes on their team are not penalized.

Asian women and Black women have fewer strong allies on their teams. They are also less likely than White women to report that senior colleagues have taken significant sponsorship actions on their behalf, such as praising their abilities or advocating for a pay raise.

Latinas and Asian women are more likely than other women of color to have colleagues' comment on their culture or nationality, such as asking where they're "really from."

Women of color and women with disabilities report more demeaning and "othering" microaggressions. They are more likely than other women to have colleagues' comment on their appearance or tell them that they "look mad" or "should smile more."

Women with disabilities frequently have their competence questioned and undermined. They are significantly more likely than other groups of women to have their expertise called into question and to have colleagues given credit for their ideas.

SWITZERLAND, INTERSECTIONALITY

In Switzerland, we recently published a White Paper on Age Diversity. The compound effect of Age Diversity overlapping with Gender Equality, LGBTQ+ Inclusion, Disability, and socio-economic diversity is astounding.

In Switzerland, approximately 60% of women aged 15 and over are employed, while 70% of men are employed, which is the average among Organization for Economic Cooperation and Development member countries (OECD).

When it comes to full- and part-time work, however, there is a significant gender gap. In every OECD-member country, more women work part-time than men; Switzerland ranks second in terms of women working part-time. Only the Netherlands has a higher proportion of women working part-time. In Switzerland, nearly 45% of all women work 30 hours or less per week, compared to 11.2% of men. In comparison to other countries, the gender gap in Switzerland is thus large.

There are even more disparities in the distribution of part-time work if you look closely. Almost one-quarter of women work less than 50% of the time, compared to 70% of men. These figures are unusual in Switzerland and will result in a significant pension gap for women as they age. In the Swiss workplace culture, mothers face a double-edged sword. More women in Switzerland are calling for an end to a workplace stigma against mothers that is impeding their careers and the country's progress.

Back to our original topic, and how age and gender intersect to the detriment of older women. Women in Switzerland earn 43% less than men, owing to the aforementioned factors (Reuters, 7 September 2022). As a result, there is a significant pension gap because women receive less pension money. This 'gender pension gap' is enormous, and women are significantly more likely to be poor in old age (www.swisslife.com).

Unfortunately, we see the same grim picture in Switzerland for people from lower socioeconomic backgrounds, where a lack of (higher) education and a lack of full-time or well-paid employment leads to discrimination and old-age poverty. Unsurprisingly, a similar compounding effect can be observed among older non-Swiss.

Finally, while conducting research for the White Paper, we discovered that, despite progress made in Switzerland for members of the LGBTQ+ community in terms of equal rights, the inclusion of LGBTQ+ older people in elder care remains a black hole. "Yet again, we are the invisible group!" said many of the people we spoke with about their experiences of aging in Switzerland.

Conclusion: Human Rights' Intersectional Future

Intersectionality in the context of human rights allows us to see how various forms of structural oppression intersect, construct, and mutually reinforce one another. Intersectionality has altered our perceptions of Diversity and Inclusion. It provides a sophisticated, comprehensive, and nuanced approach.

Diversity and inclusion are evolving from one-dimensional to multidimensional. D&I leaders and CEOs alike are encouraged to take a holistic view of their colleagues and train their respective reflexes.

QUICK SUMMARY: INTERSECTIONALITY

- The concept of intersectionality describes the ways in which systems of inequality based on gender, race, ethnicity, sexual orientation, gender identity, disability, class, and other forms of discrimination "intersect" to create unique dynamics and compounding effects
- All forms of inequality are mutually reinforcing and must therefore be analyzed and addressed simultaneously to prevent one form of inequality from reinforcing another
- Professor Kimberle Crenshaw coined the term in 1989 as a way to help explain the oppression of African American women.

ORGANIZATION

This second section of the book lays the foundation for operational D&I work:

- We introduce our *DEI operating model*, which brings together 50+ years of practical D&I experience working with global leaders and organizations
- This DEI model has proven to yield best results and has evolved over time
- By the end of this section, readers will have a thorough understanding of the seven key dimensions of D&I, how to best implement them without fear of backlash and resulting in clear and measurable results.

X. THE DEI OPERATING MODEL™

The *Bisanzio-Damchevski-Fenton DEI operating model* is built upon five pillars that drive its success:

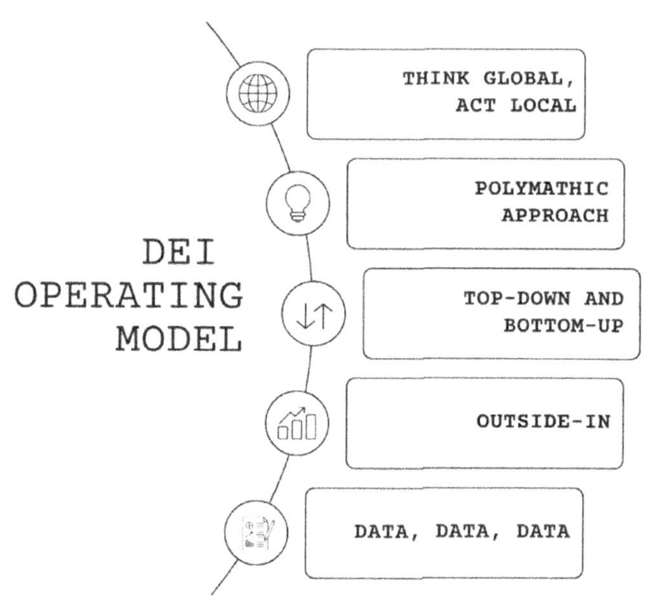

This proven DEI operating model emphasizes the need to "Think Global and Act Local" to effectively navigate diverse cultural contexts. Secondly, it encourages the development of polymaths who can consider a wide range of factors in decision-making. Thirdly, it adopts a top-down and bottom-up approach involving the CEO, leadership team, all employees, and Employee Resource Groups. Fourthly, it prioritizes an "Outside-in" perspective to stay in touch with current trends and communicate effectively. Finally, it relies heavily on data to ensure accountability, with the belief that "what doesn't get measured, doesn't get done."

XI. GENDER BALANCE

Gender Equality remains the number one priority for anyone interested or working in the field of Diversity, Equity and Inclusion. The topic is so vast, and it seems that everything has been said already.

Seven out of the top 10 *'Ted Talks'* by number of views are by women – they must be doing something right:-)

Our first message to anyone is that we are done with presenting the famous 'business case'. There is no need to quote research and science, nor will we spend time on convincing you that more women in your leadership team will be good for business. You will be glad to hear that we won't dwell on the number of incompetent men either.

Our starting point is simple: Gender Equality is a Human Right. "A gender-equal society would be one where the word *gender* does not exist: Where everyone can be themselves." (Gloria Steinem).

What are the single most impactful ways to substantially and sustainably increase the gender equality within your organization?

1. If you want to see progress, you will see progress. Promise. Start by asking yourself and your leadership team, where Gender Equality ranks on your business agenda, and this will be the exact mirror of your results.

2. Do you have clear targets, quotas or KPIs in place?

3. Who are your role models in your current and future organization?

4. Did you know that women are 'over mentored' and 'under-sponsored'?

5. Do you believe that there is a shortage of female talent? At least for some functions like IT, Sales or Engineering?

6. Are you ensuring Equal Pay and Equal Opportunity?

7. Do you know how many women at which level are leaving your organization and why?

8. How inclusive and ready is your organization to not only attract but retain key female talent?

9. What is your mechanism to hold individual leaders accountable and to track progress?

10. How senior, ready and impactful is your ERG to foster the professional development of women?

Oh Dear, more questions than answers? Here we go:

Decades of working within multinational organizations taught us that the single most differentiating factor is the willingness and the commitment from the CEO and her leadership team to make Gender Equality a key business priority. Once this is credibly in place, agreed and widely communicated, progress will begin.

GOALS, TARGETS, KPIs

What doesn't get measured, doesn't get done. This wisdom applies to Gender Equality as to any other change or progress you want to achieve. If your organization is just starting out, have someone run the data and analytics of how many women and men are at each level of your organization and where are they based. If further advanced, design and work with a dashboard to provide real life data on the more basic information correlating with age, seniority, position in the talent development matrix and whether a specific and detailed career development and succession plan is in place. As any SMART goal, your goal regarding Gender Equality needs to be realistic, achievable, specific, time sensitive and easy to measure. We here don't shy away from a quota. We may not like a quota, but we do like, what it does! A quota sets the record straight and enables positive discrimination of an equally qualified woman, as long as gender parity isn't achieved. This is codified in the majority of the Western constitutions under equality standards and the mandate not to discriminate based on sex. Once you have a baseline within your organization, set this SMART goal, target or quota, talk about it, communicate it internally and externally. Shout it from the rooftop - your competition does.

1. 'You cannot be, what you cannot see'. This in a nutshell is, why role models are so important to promote gender equality. The more charismatic, smart, successful and human female leaders you have within your organization, the more realistic it is for more junior female talent to see themselves in similar roles. Embrace what women bring to the table, hold space for them to speak up and ensure their contribution is valued as it should be ... and more women will follow. A set of talent you will want to stay engaged, now more than ever, to stay competitive.

2. Decades over decades women have been mentored by senior leaders, with very little to no results. We recommend Executive Sponsorship to move the needle. The Executive Sponsorship Program is incredibly impactful; hence we have dedicated a special chapter within this book.

3. Sorry to all search firms out there, external female talent mapping doesn't work. What does work, is filling open positions. Instead of working on creating a passive talent pool, shift your efforts to an inclusive employer branding and getting the organization ready to truly embrace and include incoming senior female talent. Implement a strategy of equal interview panels, as well as equality amongst your final candidates, who are interviewed for the open position.

4. It's hard to imagine a company in today's world getting away with paying women less for equal work. Equal Pay assessments have become common standard, if not the law. Change, before you have to. Equal Opportunity requires a much more qualitative look into your hiring process, onboarding, career progression, succession planning and talent development.

5. Learn from your exit interviews and be creative. A good practice we have seen, is reaching out by an independent provider three to six months following the departure of the so called *'regrettable'* female talent. These are high performing women with potential, who have left your company voluntarily. Why? You will not be able to find a more honest and truthful account of what it is like working for you than listening to these voices. Use this approach to gather valuable data and course correct by addressing issues raised. The amount of time and money saved due to increased retention will by far outweigh the money spent.

6. Time and time again we see this scenario: Due to amazing employer branding and a fantastic interview process you are able to hire a senior high potential woman. And the effort stops here. Remember, Inclusion is not only being invited to the party, but being asked to dance. There is really no value in hiring diverse talent, without enabling them to perform at their best and bringing their whole selves to work. This dimension is too often

overlooked and leads to frustrations for both parties and ultimately in loss of female talent down the road.

7. Advanced organizations are holding their leaders accountable by including D&I goals within their annual performance evaluation and ultimately their bonus payout. A credible and committed company will embrace this approach.

8. Your company's ERG to foster the professional development of women needs to be able to attract and to be open to men as well as women. Men are still overwhelmingly in positions of power and excluding men from these efforts will only alienate. Successes are seen, when both men and women are equally supportive and engaged when it comes to driving Gender Equality. Your ERG is a great platform to make this happen.

GENDER EQUALITY IN MEDICAL RESEARCH

As we work to promote gender equality not only in the workplace, but throughout society, let us take a moment to recognize the advances being made in medical research. Increased gender awareness in medical research has been a critical step toward greater equality and inclusion in the field of medicine. For many years, white male researchers dominated medical research, resulting in a significant bias in the development of medical treatments and disease understanding. However, there has been a growing recognition in recent years of the importance of gender equality in medical research, and gender equality is now considered a key requirement for receiving grants. This has resulted in renewed efforts to encourage more women and people from diverse backgrounds to participate in medical research. This helps to ensure that medical treatments are designed with both men's and women's needs in mind, and that they are effective and safe for all patients.

MEN ADVOCATING PROGRESS

To conclude this chapter on Gender Equality, a shout-out goes to the ever-growing number of men getting involved! In your organization, find a way to inspire and equip men to leverage their unique opportunity and responsibility to be advocates for gender equity. Create a safe and productive space, where men get engaged to enhance gender partnership and by doing so, accelerating the creation of an inclusive workspace. We are delighted to see that the role of men in D&I has grown significantly in recent years. For even more men to be effective advocates for change, we must understand gender norms and personal barriers that can undermine progress.

QUICK SUMMARY: GENDER BALANCE

- Gender Equality was made part of international human rights law by the Universal Declaration of Human Rights, which was adopted by the UN General Assembly on 10 December 1948
- Achieving full gender equality, one of the 17 Sustainable Development Goals (SDGs) could take close to 300 years if the current rate of progress continues according to the United Nations
- Organizations play a significant role by setting clear gender goals, attracting and retaining female talent, fostering career development via Executive Sponsorship, actively involving men in driving progress, ensuring Equal Pay and implementing an inclusive Family Leave policy.

XII. LGBTQ+ INCLUSION

queer : verb: to consider or interpret (something) from a perspective that rejects traditional categories of gender and sexuality.

If we look at every organization's D&I strategy, Gender Equality is with no doubt the common denominator across all businesses, nongovernmental or governmental organizations. But what comes after gender equality, is where the box of options opens up. Yourself, myself and every D&I leader asks themselves this question: "What else should be part of my D&I strategy?"

For D&I, same as every business strategy, or for that matter even for the strategy in your personal life there is one common rule: you can't have it all, and especially not at the same time. If you deceived yourself that with your business strategy you will reach everyone without a target audience, you are setting yourself up for a failure. If you deceived yourself with your personal life strategy that you will be liked by everybody you meet, you are again setting yourself up for failure. Prioritizing the D&I focus dimensions is never easy, but for many of them you can easily get the "buy-in" or build the pitch as they feel like the right thing to do. If we take for example the dimension of Disabilities, there is not a single person in any organization that will oppose the strategy and say it is wrong to focus on this underrepresented group. But this is hardly the case with every dimension we work with.

Have this in mind: you are not doing D&I right, unless it makes someone a bit **uncomfortable** in their seat.

Having said that, the award for the most "uncomfortable" D&I dimension goes undoubtedly to LGBTQ+ Inclusion. The LGBTQ+ inclusion initiatives are usually the toughest ones to crack in any organization, but if you get it right the benefits you can reap are multifaceted and indirectly affect every other dimension of Diversity & Inclusion. For that reason, the LGBTQ+ Inclusion is the "Trojan horse" of your strategy - change someone's mindset on this topic, and inclusive behavior follows on all other dimensions. The benefits are multifaceted: diversity flourishes, innovation and creativity are unleashed in the organization and the most loyal army of brand ambassadors is created.

Before we continue with the details of the chapter, it is important to pause and make a clear distinction between the terminology and acronyms used throughout the book. You probably have already noticed the term LGBTQ+ Inclusion, and you also know that the community is much larger than those five letters and a plus sign. Every member of the LGBTQQIP2SAA+ (lesbian, gay, bisexual, transgender, queer, questioning, intersex, pansexual, two-spirit (2S), androgynous, and asexual) is equally valid and worthwhile. For the sake of simplicity only and for no other reason, in this book LGBTQ+ stands as an acronym for lesbian, gay, bisexual, transgender, and the "plus" is intended as an all-encompassing representation of sexual orientations gender expressions and gender identities.

The most significant pre-requisite in reaping all these benefits is first getting your "house in order" and we will explore this action further below. Be credible and genuine in your intentions, or you will end up in an irreversible social media disaster. We are very sure that your organization is unique, and not every strategy is applicable everywhere. Before jumping into any actions, the first thing to focus on is to understand what the climate in your organizations is, and the best way to do this is via qualitative measures. Either roundtables, focus groups or reverse mentorship programs, these are all great tools that you can use to better grasp the challenges and the state of the community within an organization.

The LGBTQ+ community is often stuck in the "invisibility" realm, and one of your major objectives will be to bring it to the surface. But be ready for a battle - there almost isn't a single organization where you can easily get a unanimous global support for your LGBTQ+ efforts. And be ready to be challenged by the community - they will become your fiercest allies along the way.

Is it worth fighting for?

- Almost 3 billion people live in countries where consensual same-sex activity is criminalized.
- Being gay is punishable in 70 UN member states by imprisonment, torture or even death.
- The LGBTQ+ community has $3.7 Trillion in purchasing power.

There are reasons of the heart, and there are reasons of the mind for implementing your LGBTQ+ strategy. These three facts alone, should give you the answer. The most common question that you will always be asked: “Why”. Why is LGBTQ+ Inclusion so important to be in the top focus areas of the D&I strategy? Stay tuned, the answer is coming right up.

Why LGBTQ+ Inclusion matters is best answered via the Four Stakeholders’ model. As you go along with the strategy and building awareness, people are going to be challenging you from the first time you introduce the topic to their agendas. They all start with the basic game of numbers - total population, number of people who have self-identified, etc. Nevertheless, as you’ll get to see later - these numbers are just scratching the surface.

As you will hear us repeat this, many times throughout the book - D&I is a business strategy. But only the few really good leadership books teach you the real lesson in this data craze overloaded world. Data should be one of the inputs that make up your strategy, but data solely should not drive your decision, only provides an insight to it. Now do not get us wrong – we are not striking a war against data, in fact we are a strong believer of the “what gets measured gets done” attitude. A set of numbers measured in a limited context with no complete overview on all the factors contributing to the outcomes of those numbers cannot drive your HR or D&I strategy. Therefore, the factors contributing to the impact that the LGBTQ+ inclusion has on organizations aren’t as simple as counting the community and the population percentage of the world.

THE FOUR STAKEHOLDER MODEL:

As the name gives it away, this model consists of four stakeholders which encapsulate the major driving forces around the business case and the importance of implementing an LGBTQ+ strategy in your organization: The Community, The Allies, The Consumers and The Shareholders.

COMMUNITY

This dimension of the Four Stakeholders model is the members of the LGBTQ+ community themselves, and the reason why they matter to be part of your Diversity & Inclusion strategy is probably the most straight forward out of them all. The right to express one's sexual orientation and gender is a basic human right, based on the universality of human rights and the inalienable nature of rights belonging to every person by virtue of being human. And – it is the right thing to do.

Unfortunately, even today almost 40% of individuals decide to remain or go back in the closet once they enter the workplace and experience a significant decrease of productivity. This phenomenon is best described by the emotional tax concept. Emotional Tax is the combination of feeling different from peers at work because of gender, race, and/or ethnicity and the associated effects on health, well-being, and ability to thrive at work. In every-day life, this is often explained through the typical weekend chit-chat with your colleagues and team members: "Friday -

what are your plans for the weekend", "Monday -How did you spent the weekend" – the amount of energy and concentration a person trying to hide and cover up stories for a simple question like that can be devastating. The emotional tax destroys careers, organizations, but more importantly has a devastating impact on people's lives.

No matter in which company you work for, there is usually a fundamental non-discriminatory policy that sets the ground rules of protecting your LGBTQ+ community. But it goes much further beyond that, as policies are written words and real-life experience is something different. When your queer community flourishes at work and can be themselves, you will reap the benefits of a culture that thrives on creativity, innovation and loyalty.

ALLIES

Whenever you will be in a room full of people introducing them to the topic of LGBTQ+ Inclusion, whether it is an auditorium setting or a practical workshop, this stakeholder is explained with a very simple exercise. Ask everyone to stand up or raise their hand if they have a close friend, colleague or a family member that is part of the community. And then, watch what happens – in most of the cases at least 80% of the people in the room raise their hands. When the participants look around it is immediately evident that the LGBTQ+ community together with their Allies network, creates a large and quite powerful representation of your employees.

If there is anything you should note down and always remember from this section, it is that the only way to have a successful LGBTQ+ strategy is by having the allies on your side. They are the catalyst and the ambassador for the change you wish to see upon your organization. In 2023 more than ever, we done with trying to fix the marginalized group members, making them more confident, asking them to lean in and raise their hand. It is time now for everyone around them to step up their game and join the fight for equality, because they are the majority indeed, and they are the ones who can change the culture we work in, to an open-minded environment where you can be yourself.

The concept of an Ally revolves around the idea of understanding someone who is not like you and does not suffer the same oppressions, but who supports your struggle for rights and freedom. Often, allies find their inner calling in fighting for a bigger cause and feel empowered to speak up for the fair treatment of others. This is becoming one of the strongest motivational instinct that you can utilize in your strategies and it is a clear sign of a true partner in driving your agenda forward. And if you think you are too small to make an impact, try going to bed with a mosquito in the room.

CONSUMERS

There are two types of great power that the LGBTQ+ consumers possess: influential and financial. If you are "in" for the biggest social media disaster that your brands and your company will face, you are at the right place, as

just a tiny public error towards LGBTQ+ injustice coming from the messages your company or your products are broadcasting, and you are done. Remember the example of Guido Barilla in the first chapter?
On the flip side, if you authentically engage with the community, they become your loudest troop of ambassadors. For the readers with the marketing hat on them, LGBTQ+ consumers represent a large group of the early-adopters consumer demographic, an audience seen as innovators and trendsetters.
In the US alone, the financial power of the LGBTQ+ community is capped at 720 billion dollars. Quite the hefty amount, isn't it? That is a number that can turn any marketer's or a CEO's eyeballs into dollar signs instantly. Not so fast though. The biggest mistake you can make as a company is to try utilizing the power of the community for your financial gains only. It is very easy to stick a rainbow on your products for a month and wait to reap the benefits. But the LGBTQ+ people are identifying with their sexuality and their gender every day of their lives, not just during a limited commercial campaign, once per year. This is a concept known as "pink washing", but more about it later. If your LGBTQ+ consumers believe in what your brand stands for, you've got yourselves a loyal consumer base for a lifetime.

SHAREHOLDERS

This is the last of the four stakeholders in the business case of LGBTQ+ inclusion, but certainly not the least. During a business valuation, the financials analysts using a set of procedures are estimating the economic value of one organization. For quite some time the criteria were pretty standard and related directly to financial results and investments - until recently that is. But recently more coming from the abundance of studies and evidence, Diversity & Inclusion is part of the evaluation criteria of the valuation and in particular LGBTQ+ inclusion measurements are carefully observed by the analysts. This is explained by the link between high performing companies who thrive on innovation and their successfully delivered LGBTQ+ strategies. And of course - the higher the estimate and scoring out of this analysis, the higher the shareholders' value.

A win-win for everyone, wouldn't you agree?

GLOBAL STRATEGY

As nowadays it is often the case, purposefully or not, many brands and organizations are establishing a global presence. This is in major part driven by globalization and the digital age, as you can go viral in the world over night. The international presence of one organization of course has to be supported by growing local branches or local mergers and acquisitions, which can help you penetrate the market and develop a targeted strategy - think globally, act locally.
The international presence particularly of major organizations is a godsend, yet nothing comes without a price, or without a challenge to say the least. When you look at this aspect with the D&I lenses, you are faced with multiple layers of diversity which can hurt you, if you don't have an intentional strategy in place. Different cultures,

different nationalities, climates, different belief systems and different religions, and very important - different laws and regulations. Just to make it a bit more real, lets now remove one more layer of the peeled onion and imagine your global LGBTQ+ inclusion strategy within a branch of your organization in the Middle East. This situation is unfortunately not just a rare exception, but the reality of your global LGBTQ+ Inclusion strategy. In order to be adequately addressed, there are three models of engagement for international organizations in the matters of LGBTQ+ inclusion: “When in Rome”; “Embassy” and the “Advocate” model.

WHEN IN ROME (do as Romans do)

The *When in Rome* model is the earliest stage in which one company can find itself on the LGBTQ+ Inclusion journey. As the saying goes, this is where you almost don’t take any action at all. To be perfectly honest with you, it is very easy to say your organization is at this stage and remain in the comfort zone, but in reality, most organizations can easily skip it and go to the next one. Perform a risk assessment to make sure it is not damaging your business, and then decide to take the first actions for the next level. The When in Rome model is ultimately not good for your organization and your people and certainly not good for business. It almost equalizes your company with a “neutral” view on the matter, and at today’s state of the world, your organization cannot afford to be seen as neutral when your people are at stake.

EMBASSY

In the "Embassy" model, you create an inclusive workplace internally for your LGBTQ+ employees no matter where the locations are, although outside of the walls of the organization, the environment might be different. A term which you need to get used go and it will never go out of fashion is "**safe haven**". A state of your organizational culture and environment you should aim for, where every single one of your employees will feel respected and protected at work, no matter the geographical location. The best strategy in this phase is implementing global guidelines and policies, leaving space for further local calibration in order to adhere to the regulations. The notion of inclusion and equality can be your trojan horse and the platform under which you will embed LGBTQ+ Inclusion and raise awareness even in places known as the "red zones" in the world from the annual ILGA reports. During this stage, expect to be challenged even in the interpretation of the local laws and regulations, in terms of what is forbidden and what isn't, but don't give up these fights just because someone is waving a law book that they haven't properly read. Many times, these laws need a profounder understanding of what is at stake, and it is often not as black and white as it is perceived. Take the example of Russia and their sadly famous anti-gay law. When you, as a D&I professional, will have a first look at the issue, the immediate response you will get is a clear NO, the law is the law and there is nothing you can do. But find yourself a lawyer friend at your company and start digging deeper. As it turns out, the anti-gay law in Russia is in fact anti propaganda towards minors only. And while being far from happy news, it reveals that there is still a lot you can achieve as an organization, as workplaces are exclusively adults only environments and so on, all while never breaking the law. Remember, this model is the one where most companies should fall nowadays, but they shouldn't remain there for too long.

ADVOCATE

As you might be guessing already, this is the most advanced stage of your LGBTQ+ inclusion journey and it is the final state towards which we are aiming. It is based on the principles that your organization has been matured from the previous two stages and now it is actively advocating for LGBTQ+ rights in the public sphere. This strategy is particularly impactful in the developing countries where the laws are lacking behind the norms of the society, or even worse – they are going backwards. What you should take-away from the Advocate stage is that we are stronger together. These activities are only successful and best carried out if you put aside the competition and work together with other organizations to make a joint plan of changing the climate in a particular country together. In 2019, the country of Brunei introduced a strict law of death penalties for the LGBTQ+ community, but this wasn't well received neither by private organizations, neither by governmental entities. They all took a public stance against the new law in Brunei, cancelling their business with the country leader and his business affairs, and soon after – the death penalty law was removed. You see, pushing the envelope further in defending the fundamental human rights and saving lives will be the most rewarding part of your job and reveals the power organizations have in the society.

GET YOUR HOUSE IN ORDER

Let's see: You have the business case, the international strategy, you got the gist of where the organization stands and – you got yourself a powerful executive sponsor. Now it is time to roll up your sleeves and get cracking.

Ask yourself these questions: is my house in order? Will you in reality invite people over or put your lovely home on your social media feed if you have no sink or haven't cleaned the house in months? Most probably not, as neither would I. Getting your house in order in the context of your LGBTQ+ strategy means you need to look at policies, guidelines, procedures and manuals. Is it the most fun and outgoing activity – not at first. But you will have fun as you start digging and seeing the gaps. You just can't make it further in your journey if you don't get the basics right, just look at this as writing the laws in a country in the most inclusive possible way. This activity is the homework of the D&I team, together with your colleagues in the other HR teams like Compensation and Benefits, International Mobility, Compliance, etc. Every policy should be double checked for its inclusivity: for example, the ones where we have worked on are: Code of conduct coverage; Family leave for adoption and surrogacy parents; Partner health insurance; LGBT Travel Safety Policies and Guidelines; International mobility support policies; etc.

ERG – EMPLOYEE RESOURCE GROUP

This is one of the must actions in any organization and to be perfectly blunt, always gets mistaken for having a strategy in place. It is clearly far from enough and it is only a red flag that unfortunately, those organizations do not take LGBTQ+ inclusion seriously. As its name suggests, it is very important for this affinity group to be Employee led and to be formed organically out of the few employees who show the most enthusiasm. The most successful ERGs have a guiding document, such as terms of reference, which clearly defines the purpose of the group, how the success is measured and especially its leadership structure. Every ERG needs to have 1-2 Chairpersons, Comms Persons and Budget person.

TRANSGENDER, GENDER IDENTITY & GENDER EXPRESSION

As pre-empted in the Evolution of D&I, the often-forgotten T stands for Transgender, not for "**Too difficult to deal with**". On the contrary, trans* and non-binary trajectories expose us to the possibility of resisting a model that does not correspond to us in order to live our own truth. People who have lived or are living a transidentitarian trajectory have a sufficient self-consciousness and an ability to express how they want to be, because identity is also constructed by the look of others. Instead of trying to include them in a binary way of thinking, perhaps we can learn from them to make our way of thinking more human, more plural, even more creative. Let's go to the basics.

Gender identity refers to how a person feels about their identity. It answers the question, how do I feel in my own body? It is an internal sense of being male, female, both, neither, or something else entirely. It may or may not correspond to the sex assigned at birth by the medical team. A person who does not identify with the gender assigned at birth is defined as a trans* person, trans binary or trans non-binary. Trans is an adjective, not a noun, because defining a person only by their gender identity is dehumanizing. A person who identifies in the gender assigned at birth is said to be cisgender.

Gender expression, on the other hand, refers to the way a person presents their gender to the world through their behavior, clothing, hairstyle, voice, and other characteristics. Gender expression can be masculine, feminine, or androgynous, and can vary over time or in different situations, according to what is culturally and historically defined. Remember that not so long ago, men wore dresses and heels were invented for men to wear. It is not a direct reflection of a person's gender identity and may or may not conform to societal expectations or norms.

If this sounds a bit confusing, consider the following example: gender identity is the painting canvas and gender expression is the painting. It is possible to alter a painting by changing its canvas and neither the painting nor the gender expression is dependent on the other. For example, if my painting is rectangular in shape, it does not mean that I have to use only the color blue.

It's important to note that gender identity and gender expression are not the same as biological sex, which refers to a person's physical and biological characteristics. Understanding and respecting people's gender identity and gender expression is a critical part of creating a more inclusive and equitable society for all people, regardless of their gender identity.

But perhaps, a revelation that has come to us quite recently is the connection of transgender rights and the lack of progress in gender equality, in the traditional sense. Hear us out.

The difficulties transgender people confront in the workplace are emblematic of deeper issues of sexism and heterosexism in mainstream business. The lived experiences of transgender persons have the potential to shake up conventional ideas about gender and inspire a broader conception of what it means to be a “man” or a “woman”. What it means to lead like a man or lead like a woman. We are stuck in the binarity of genders, trying to equalize and compare men to women, and we end up in a place where women act like men to get a seat at the table, unconsciously replicating the same problematic behavior of oppressive, heteronormative and sexist systems.

Saying it bluntly, when your CEO understands the fluidity of gender, its construction and its deconstruction of what we think it takes to be a man or a woman, we might end up in a world where there are no men VS women, and maybe, just maybe, we will realize that we are all more or less gender fluid. And that is a wonderful celebration that puts gender in the center, not to divide us, but to empower us.

For example, the first answer that comes when searching for feminine leadership traits is empathy. You have or are a CEO who identifies as a man, and you are empathic. What could this possibly mean? Going to leave you with that as food for thought.

Focusing on this topic can help us break down traditional gender norms and expectations that are harmful to people of all genders, including those who identify as cisgender. We will be able to establish a society that is more welcoming for people of all genders if we recognize the presence of non-binary and gender non-conforming individuals and provide support for them. We recognize that ideas about gender have been molded by the history, vary depending on the setting, and develop with time; we welcome this development as an opportunity to learn from the people, organizations, and causes that have inspired and motivated us to become better sponsors of their work. That gender nonconformity is not a foreign notion but embedded in our cultures around the world, that recognizing all identities is crucial to the future of our society, and that the gender we were assigned at birth doesn't decide our story, are all things they are helping the rest of us to see. It's time to not just rewrite history to include people of all gender identities and expressions, but to also reimagine what it means to be human.

BAD PRACTICES

Finally, we would love to close the chapter with a few notes on what is not recommendable to do in this sphere. Please stay as far away as possible from these initiatives and just do the right thing.

- Pink washing – this term is gaining lots of popularity lately, as there are many organizations nowadays who rush into the LGBTQ+ consumer and appearing to only be interested in the profit gains. The right approach here is to first align the culture and gain the employees trust internally, before going publicly to claim your pride.

- Forced coming out – your employees should be voluntarily sharing with no pressure from the organization.

- Community counting - quantitatively trying to measure the size of the community in the organization especially in the beginning stages is a risky strategy and its only recommended for advanced level organizations in the matter.

QUICK SUMMARY: LGBTQ+ INCLUSION

- LGBTQ+ is an abbreviation for lesbian, gay, bisexual, transgender, queer, or questioning
- Rights affecting lesbian, gay, bisexual, transgender and queer people vary greatly by country or jurisdiction - encompassing everything from the legal recognition of same-sex marriage to the death penalty for homosexuality
- Organizations can help advance LGBTQ+ Inclusion around the world by applying the "Embassy" model, where they create an inclusive workplace internally for their LGBTQ+ colleagues without seeking to change laws or societal attitudes
- T stands for Transgender, not Too difficult to deal with.

XIII. AGE DIVERSITY

Japan, Germany, Switzerland, Italy, the US, Belgium, the UK... are all heading in the same direction and that is why we are saying that the next big topic in D&I will be Age Diversity. By a far margin that is!

Population ageing is profoundly changing the workplace. The coming decades will be marked by strong demographic changes. Since 2010, the large baby boomer cohorts have been reaching older ages and successive generations are of smaller size or grow at a slower pace. By 2050 the OECD predicts, the share of population aged 50 and older will increase from 37% in 2020 to 45% on average (www.oecd-library.org). Similarly, the old-age dependency ratio - a demographic indicator that measures the size of the population aged 65 and over relative to that of people at classic working ages 20-64 - is projected to increase by two-thirds in OECD economies, from 30% in 2020 to 50% in 2050. Many countries with a comparatively young population structure today, like Chile, Korea or the Slovak Republic will face a particularly strong transformation process.

These demographic trends are working in favor of multigenerational workplaces with a greater mix of workers at all ages rather than a pyramid of much larger numbers of younger workers and relatively few older workers. This diversity of experiences, generations and skills mix brings several benefits to the workplace.

However, today, large companies with more than 250 employees report that only 6% of their employees are above age 64 according to AARP's 2020 Global Employer Survey. This could rise substantially in the coming decades if companies' recruitment would follow the change in the age composition of the adult population. Workplaces will change their faces and employers will have to adapt their HR strategies and workplace practices accordingly.

In the medium-term, demographic change may lead to labor shortages reported already in pre-COVID-19 times. The COVID-19 crisis has led to massive turbulence on labor markets across all OECD countries from the second quarter of 2020. Unemployment rates have surged and numbers of workers under short-term compensation schemes have skyrocketed in some countries, with disruptive consequences for economies.

In the short to medium term, labor markets will need to recover from this sudden shock, which may temporarily put a halt to the labor shortages or change sectors in which they appear. However, the crisis will not change the long-term dynamics induced by demographic change, which primarily work through the supply-side of the labor market. The pressure to react to population ageing and low fertility rates will hence prevail. Therefore, the demographic transition may, in the medium to long term, reinforce rising labor shortages.

Offsetting this trend by longer working lives would need very big efforts by countries and companies.

Enough of the facts & figures. What are the threats and – more interestingly – opportunities for societies at large and the workplace in particular? As often in life, the biggest threat is to do nothing. My advice to any organization and D&I teams is simply: change, before you have to.

We are heading from three, to four, to five generations in the workplace. Let's take a closer look at both 'bookends'; namely the generation 50plus as well as Gen Z.

GEN Z

Gen Z: the workers who want it all? Really? Harvard Business Review summarizes in an article published on 03 June 2020 by Lauren Stiller Rikleen that members of Gen Z were just beginning their career journeys when they were furloughed or fired as the pandemic escalated and economies shut down. Those still in school were suddenly confined to their homes. Collectively, this group is experiencing the greatest national trauma since the Great Depression and World War II just as they are starting out in the world. For the workforce to be equipped to move forward and thrive, employers will need to address the fallout resulting from COVID-19 on their youngest – and future – employees. There are three main areas companies should focus on to support this generation: skill development, which was interrupted as colleges and universities shifted to online learning: stress management, something this generation was already struggling with before the pandemic; and emotional intelligence, a skill that Gen Z may not have fully developed due to massive interruption in their ability to discover what motivates and fulfills them.

Gen Z is now the largest emerging workforce. This young, digital-intuitive generation accounts for roughly 90 million people in the US alone, and many are ready and willing to work - but in their terms. Gen Z, those born between 1997 - 2010, is the first generation to be born into a world of digital technology, thus earning the nickname 'Zoomer'. Unsurprisingly, they are the most tech-savvy generation. People in this generation value experiences over possessions, keep their eye on the prize, and are fiercely independent. This is a true come-as-you-are-generation believing in equality, respect and a healthy competition.

Nearly one-third of all Gen Zer's turned 18 in 2020, making them the youngest generation in the workforce today. It's estimated that they now make up close to a quarter of the global workforce. Though they may be young, this generation is characterized as being self-starters who aren't afraid to ask questions if needed. While Gen Z isn't afraid to throw in the work to move quickly and take advantage of career growth opportunities, they also value a healthy work-life-blend and understand the importance of mental health - arguably more than any generation before them. Gen-Zer's also tend to have zero shame when it comes to job hopping.

If a job isn't checking all the boxes for them, they'll find a new one that does. For you as working for an employer seeking to attract and retain this talented group of people, we put together a list, of what they are looking for:

1) *Diversity* - Generation Z workers are clued-in to Inclusion and are more likely to consider working for a company with a proven track record of Diversity in the workplace that hires people from different cultures, socio-economic backgrounds, religions and genders.

2) *Stability* - After growing up in the financial aftermath of 2008 and now entering the workforce during an economic slump, Gen Z workers are hyper aware of the importance of a stable job - even if they tend to be job hoppers. This is a frugal generation, and jobs that offer financial stability are key.

3) *Company responsibility* - Companies that are aware of their responsibility to workers and the world outside of their company are big draws for Gen Z. Responsibility can come in the form of true respect, fair treatment, and equity for employees, to being active in social justice initiatives both locally and globally.

4) *Work-life blend* - This generation watched their parents and grandparents struggle and work themselves to the bone, and they've seen the effects. Companies not just offering career growth opportunities but also good work-life blend appeal to them. This may be found through benefits such as

unlimited vacation days, four-day-workweeks or simply a positive work culture.

5) *Transparency* – Since authenticity is important to Gen Z, they expect the companies they work for to be transparent. They want to know details – even if the truth isn't perfect. They are interested in pay equity, where the money goes and to whom, and the integrity of the company they are investing time into.

6) *Flexibility* – Being flexible caters to Gen Z's desire for independence and work-life blend. They are interested in companies that are open to allowing them to work in the ways and from the places of their choosing that will make them more productive. Ideally, these would be offices that offers human interaction coupled with the option to work remotely.

By offering the above to current and future employees, you will not only be an attractive employer for Gen Z, but for all employees working in your organization. In our view the expectations will drive a more diverse and inclusive workplace and we already see Gen Z colleagues as our biggest advocates.

50PLUS

Today, life is lived in four quarters. Twenty-five years each. 0 to 25 years of age is your first quarter, 25 to 50 years old is your second, 50 to 75 is your third, and 75 to

100 is your fourth. Life expectancy is on the rise. Not only do we live longer, but we also lead healthier lives. Longevity is all the rage, and this includes the workplace.

As established above, there is an ever-increasing labor shortage and the age group 50plus is an untapped pool of labor. They are here in their third quarter, ready to contribute, advise, share and pass along their expertise and knowledge, mostly able and keen to contribute.

What can companies do?

1) Embed the ageing workforce in the corporate strategy

The first step is to prioritize the issue. Only companies that focus on older workers as a key part of their overall strategy will be able to fully utilize the existing untapped potential. The strategic embedding of better integration and continued employment of older workers much be accompanied by clear indicators. Companies should set specific targets, for example indicating the proportion of older workers they intent to employ beyond retirement age. Incentives should also be used as a means of demonstrating success. This would be similar to the approach currently taken to protect and increase diversity in company workforces for i.e., more women in leadership roles.

2) Make changes to the corporate culture by raising managers' awareness

As well as embedding this issue in their strategy, companies need to change fundamentally their corporate culture and managers' mindsets. The attitude that older workers are more expensive and perform less well than younger workers, and that employing them has more disadvantages than advantages is still common. In companies, where prejudices of this kind are widespread among both managers and HR departments, older workers are given little encouragement to continue working. While we haven't been able to find any research confirming the bias that older workers are less productive, we did come across data that confirms both HR departments and leaders perceive older workers as a disadvantage when it comes to the competitiveness of the organization. This shift in mindset and culture will not come automatically and needs to be proactively encouraged.

3) Implement strategic HR planning

Once the above is done and both the issue of older workers is embedded in the corporate strategy and steps are under way to make changes in the corporate culture, the next step is to anchor the efforts in the strategic HR Headcount planning. Similar to the approach to let's say improving gender diversity, it all starts with robust data collection and analytics. The company needs to get familiar with the age and skills profile of its workforce. Those departments or functions that are facing a future labor shortage of older workers with the potential to close gaps by keeping older workers and asking them to continue working beyond 50plus of age. This strategic planning is best done 'on the ground' involving line managers and HR Business

Partners, who have the knowledge to assess the skillset required and the proximity to the older employees to discuss the individual career planning.

4) Put specific measures in place

Once you have ticked all the boxes, now is the time to implement specific, individual measures that will help to keep older employees working for longer. These will include:

- Adapt employment models, we like job-sharing☺
- Adapt job roles
- Adapt working conditions
- Set up cross-generational teams
- Invest in Health & Wellbeing initiatives
- Review pension plan contributions

5) Foster the dialogue with employees and across generations

Here your ERG, fostering all generations at work, can play a critical role. Closing a potential generational divide as well as bringing unique 50plus challenges to the surface. As retirement and pre-retirement are top-of-mind for older workers, involving the Compensation & Benefits team is crucial. It is important that these discussions take place before the employee reaches the age of 60. Including spouses, and partners, for example through briefings is very smart, as employees often agree their retirement plans with their spouses and partners.

We were quite surprised to see that according to our research, almost 50% of those, who already retired, would have been willing to work longer, if their employer had approached them in good time and had discussed the opportunities with them (Deloitte, 'Workers wanted: how the 50plus age group can help tackle the looming labour shortage').

In closing, we would like to bring to your attention the topic of 'intersectionality'. In the context of D&I, intersectionality describes the interconnected relationship of social categorization (such as Race, Gender and Sexual Orientation) as applied to an individual group. With the generation 50plus, we have come across numerous instances of intersectionality. Namely, the financial disadvantage of older women when it comes to their financial gap in retirement fonds as they very often work part-time, have gaps in their employment due to caring for children or the elder. Equally, elder care facilities are rarely equipped to cater for the unique requirements of the LGBTQ+ community. Very often citizens from a poor socio-economic background are hit twice as hard in old age. These are urgent dimensions society and government will have to grapple with.

QUICK SUMMARY: AGE DIVERSITY

- The age diversity definition is simply "the acceptance of employees of different ages in the workplace". Age-based diversity is similar to generational diversity in that it seeks to combat age discrimination
- There are four main generations who are currently active in today's workforce: Baby Boomers, Generation X, Millennials (e.g., Generation Y) and Generation Z
- Employers must understand that each of these generations has different strengths, preferences, and work styles that are determined by the world in which they grew up, their life stage, and their professional experience.

XIV. WELLBEING AND MENTAL HEALTH

Have you already considered appointing a *Chief Happiness Officer*? Is someone in your organization looking after the Wellbeing and Mental Health of your employees? Are you offering Mindfulness and Yoga classes? If so, you are in good company and doing the right thing.

We know, we all get tired of hearing, how much the Covid pandemic has changed the workplace. Here it is true though! Parallel to the New Ways of Working, your company has either already had a robust Wellbeing strategy in place, before the pandemic and has dramatically accelerated since, or you certainly have more leaders engaged in topics like Wellbeing, Wellness, Resilience and Mental Health than ever before.

Each year, October 10 marks World Mental Health Day. From addiction to dementia to schizophrenia, almost 1 billion people worldwide suffer from a mental disorder. Lost productivity because of two of the most common mental disorders, anxiety and depression, costs the global economy US$ 1 trillion each year. In total, poor mental health was estimated to cost the world economy approximately $2·5 trillion per year in poor health and reduced productivity in 2010, a cost projected to rise to $6 trillion by 2030.

The World Health Organization (WHO) defines Mental Health as a 'state of Wellbeing in which the individual realizes his or her abilities, can cope with the normal stresses of life, work productively and fruitfully, and is able to make a contribution to his or her community'.

As we can see, a pretty important responsibility lies on the shoulder of the employer. However, there is also a substantial financial benefit attached. For example, a study by the Institute for Healthcare Consumerism concludes that organizations with effective wellness programs realize an average $5.93 in savings for every dollar spent. Such programs reduce health costs by 26%, sick days by 28% and workers' compensation and disability claims by 30%, it reports on 6 April 2022.

Never have we discussed our physical and mental health so openly and relentlessly in the workplace.

Here is a summary of the good practices we have seen and which we want to continue to see in the workplace:

1. Keeping things personal and allowing for a conversation between employee and boss that goes beyond ticking off agenda items around projects, SMART goals and how to achieve them.
2. Creating space for Learning and Sharing in the space of Wellbeing, Mental Health and Resilience via external and internal speakers and trainings.
3. Offering Mindfulness Sessions and demystifying Meditation.
4. Ensuring that employees have sufficient time for breaks in between meetings to reset.

5. Bringing in the experts, i.e., psychologists, to train and explain the early symptoms of depression, burnout, addiction and psychosis. Here we can wholeheartedly recommend ensa (https://ensa.swiss).
6. Including a set of questions around Wellbeing and Mental Health in your annual employee survey and commit to actions.

In a nutshell, less is more. The key is not to flood the organization with scattered initiatives. What employees and managers alike are looking for, is genuine interest and care. We don't adjust the workplace, but us to the workplace. Asking a person with mental health related issues to do so, is like suggesting to someone with Diabetes "Come on, make your pancreas work better!".

The positive tone is set at the top of the organization. Authentic messaging and role modeling from senior leaders is paramount. We have seen several global CEOs, who stand out by sharing their own meditation practice, resilience hacks or similar.

Given the substantive financial and non-financial benefits, we expect this positive trend to continue. If your organization hasn't yet defined a clear Wellbeing and Mental Health strategy, we highly recommend doing so.

QUICK SUMMARY: WELLBEING & MENTAL HEALTH

- The World Health Organization (WHO) describes mental health as a 'state of wellbeing in which every individual realizes their own potential, can cope with the normal stresses of life, and can work productively and fruitfully
- The COVID-19 pandemic has shown why employers must prioritize Wellbeing & Mental Health
- Companies are investing into Wellbeing & Mental Health to increase productivity and improved work performance, reduced absenteeism, turnover and injuries, and enhanced reputation increasing recruitment and retention. Improved Mental Health also benefits overall Health.

XV. SOCIOECONOMIC INCLUSION

Think socioeconomic Diversity & Inclusion in the workplace can be ignored? Think again. As the talent landscape evolves, traditional education such as university degrees are losing relevance according to Max Wessel, Chief Learning Officer at SAP. We were thrilled to hear that in the tech sector there's a considerable mind shift. STEM jobs have historically been inaccessible to all sorts of members of the world's workforce.

In this chapter, we address:

- Why it makes sense to recruit top talent from across society, rather than competing with blue-chip companies to hire from a narrow pool of like-minded candidates
- The challenges of combatting a deep-seated desire to conform, which leads to a tyranny of 'fit', a misrecognition of merit, and a tendency for social class to be self-sustaining
- How we can start cracking the 'class ceiling' to make the workplace more socioeconomically diverse and inclusive

What do we mean, when we speak about socioeconomic factors? There are five defining factors: occupation, education, income, wealth and where someone lives.

In 2020, the UK has launched a taskforce in a move to improve socioeconomic diversity at senior levels in financial and professional services. This is just another example of an initiative in the private sector to monitor diversity of workplaces and support talented people from all backgrounds in reaching their full potential. Overlooking socioeconomic diversity is no longer an option for investors. Like in the Tech-Sector, this initiative was long overdue as research carried out by Bridge Group, a non-profit consultancy that uses research to promote social equality, shows. According to their research in 2020, almost nine out of 10 senior roles in Financial Services in the UK are held by people from higher socioeconomic backgrounds.

Just ten percent of white British people from working-class backgrounds attain high-status jobs, while in the US, recent research found workers from lower social-class origins are 32 percent less likely to become managers than people from higher origins, an even greater gap than for gender (27 percent) or race (25 percent).

A similar situation in Germany. DW (Deutsche Welle) writes on 31 May 2022: "Social class: Germany's forgotten career hurdle – Today many German companies support Diversity in the workplace and are making efforts to create better opportunities for women and people of color. But socioeconomic background is a factor that often goes overlooked."

"Even when individuals from working-class backgrounds are successful in entering the country's elite occupations, they go on to earn, on average, 16 percent less than colleagues from more privileged backgrounds," wrote Sam Friedman and Daniel Laurison, authors of The Class Ceiling. "More significantly, this class pay gap is not explained away by conventional indicators of 'merit'. A substantial gap remains even when we consider a person's educational credentials, the hours they work and their level of training and experience."

The socioeconomic background plays a key role in determining which academic and professional opportunities are available — and how much discrimination a person will face in their career. Discrimination starts early in most countries. More than 80% of children whose parents went to university finish with the highest degree of secondary school, usually a precursor to university. For children from families with less formal education, it's not even half.

Yet, socioeconomic diversity is only just starting to be considered as part of companies' D&I initiatives, both because it is a less visible trait than gender or ethnicity, meaning it is easy to overlook, and because – shockingly – discrimination based on class tends to remain socially accepted to this day. Furthermore, those that do make it into the workplace often hide their origins and adopt social codes of the majority to blend in. In many ways this leads to social mobility being invisible and working-class people who come into professions like law or finance tend to assimilate and by doing so, get completely lost.

For the 'trained D&I eye', this immediately rings a bell and strongly resembles what we have heard repeatedly from the LGBTQ+ community: "We are the invisible group!". Thanks to impressive progress made with regards to closing this visibility-gap, there is a lot of work to do when it comes to promoting and fostering a workplace that is inclusive of the socioeconomic background. Imagine the anger and hopelessness felt by employees, who see a lot of attention and energy going towards LGBTQ+ Inclusion as well as Mental Health and nowhere to turn to for their issues.

In a modern and civilized society, there should be no link between educational opportunities and family income, so that all (young) people are given the chance to fulfill their potential – regardless of their family background, school or where they live.

1. The business case for socioeconomic Inclusion

Increased productivity in the workplace: business benefits from social inclusion in several ways: diversity can be a source of creativity and innovation, lifting productivity, social inclusion can also lift profitability and help target market segments.

Improved employment outcomes: greater social inclusion means people are less likely to experience discrimination-based adversity, and less likely to experience discrimination in the first place, increasing their capacity to seek employment or gain longer working hours and contribute to the economy.

Improvement of mental and physical health: social inclusion can counteract isolation and increase community participation, which helps to alleviate health problems, especially mental health issues such as anxiety, addiction and depression.

Reduced cost of social services: social inclusion reduces the cost of social services, welfare or unemployment benefits by easing pressure on the public sector and reducing the need for income and housing support payments.

Inclusive growth: by lifting wages and workforce participation in geographical areas of socio-economic disadvantages, the benefits of economic growth can be shared more evenly across communities.

2. The crux with the 'Class Ceiling'

In their book 'The Class Ceiling - Why it Pays to be Privileged', the authors Sam Friedman and Daniel Laurison, uncover what affects whether you get promoted. They convincingly argue that it isn't just your ability. Social mobility is not a myth, but meritocracy is a sham. It is possible, though difficult, to come from a working-class background and enter the elite professions, but, as sociologists they point out in their study that you will find it harder to progress and you'll earn less money, even when you have the same degree from the same university as someone with more privileged beginnings. They are quite specific, on average, in fact, you'll earn GBP 7'000 a year less.

The writer Annete Kuhn puts it ever so elegantly, when she says: "Class is something beneath your clothes, under your skin, in your reflexes, your psyche, at the very core of your being".

3. How to crack the 'Class Ceiling'

Many organizations just recently added socioeconomic inclusion to their D&I agenda. To be truly inclusive, they claim, you must look at the disadvantages faced by individuals from certain socioeconomic backgrounds and produce a plan to address this difference. It is about time that this underappreciated element of Diversity & Inclusion finds its way into the boardroom.

Here are good practices, we have seen so far:

- Start by a better understanding of the make-up of your workforce. *Barclays* now asks their employees in their 'Your View' survey to share their socioeconomic background and includes a question from the Social Mobility Commission / Foundation: 'What was the occupation of your main household earner when you were aged at about 14?'. Brilliant!

- Several companies have initiated their respective ERG, which aim to amplify the voices of their colleagues and help to learn about the impact that socioeconomic background can have on colleagues in the workplace. This will create better transparency for all employees, the needs of colleagues and clients, whilst strategically contributing to business objectives and advocating for socioeconomic inclusion.

- Review, Focus, sharpen your efforts in recruitment and talent attraction. We have come across successful *employability programs*, where candidates are supported by organizations to increase their individual employability through workshops. Or follow the example of SAP and revisit your barriers to entry by relaxing requirements around formal education.

QUICK SUMMARY: SOCIO-ECONOMIC INCLUSION

- The socioeconomic status is a characterization derived from a "combination of education, income and occupation", and can seriously impact wellbeing and career opportunities
- Creating a socially diverse workforce is about removing barriers of entry ("class ceiling") and creating social mobility
- In place of four-year-degrees, many organizations are instead focusing on skills-based hiring to widen the talent pool.

XVI. RACE & ETHNICITY

Within two weeks of the killing of George Floyd, George Floyd protests erupted in the US and around the world. In fact, the demonstrations were more diverse than the 2017 fall racial justice march and previous moments of protest in the Black Lives Matter and civil rights movements. The brutal police killings of George Floyd and other African Americans in 2020 marked a turning point in global awareness of racial injustice and its impact on life outcomes. Amid protests around the world following the killing of George Floyd in May 2020, organizations around the world re-awakened or woke up to the topic of Race & Ethnicity. For US companies operating outside of the US, this trend has continued until today.

For us as D&I Leaders in Europe, the topic of Race & Ethnicity remains highly complex and brings several challenges. In fact, already at the level of simply defining, what Race & Ethnicity means in Continental Europe, EMEA or Asia Pacific and Japan, is unique and needs to be addressed mindfully and in the given context. Here the approach of 'one size fits all' reaches its limits.

EUROPE

The total number of national minority populations in Europe is estimated at 105 million people, or 14% of 770 million Europeans. The Russians are the most populous among Europeans, with a population over 135 million. There are not universally accepted and precise definitions of the terms "ethnic group" and "nationality". In the context of European ethnography in particular, the terms *ethnic group*, *people*, *nationality* and *ethno-linguistic group*, are used as mostly synonymous, although preference may vary in usage with respect to the situation specific to the individual countries of Europe.

SWITZERLAND

At the end of 2021, the percentage of foreigners living in Switzerland was at 25,7%, 0.2% above previous years. In numbers this means that 2.24 million foreigners are living in Switzerland out of 8,6 million in total. In an international city like Geneva, the percentage of foreigners are the highest with 40,5% at the end of 2021. Switzerland is one of the countries with the highest percentage of foreigners and far ahead of Germany with 12%, the UK 11%, Spain 6,8% or France at 6%.

The largest percentage of foreigners living in Switzerland is from Italy, followed by Germany, Portugal, France, Kosovo, Spain, Turkey, North Macedonia, Serbia and finally Austria. The total number of Black African living in Switzerland was approximately 100'000 at the end of 2021.

JAPAN

Is Japan a monoculture? *Yes.* 99% of people who live in Japan are ethnically Japanese and embrace Japanese culture. There is a small minority of South Korean people and a very small number of Chinese people living in Japan. Rather than the suppression of different ethnic groups within a given society, sometimes monoculturalism manifests as the active preservation of a country's national culture via the exclusion of external influences. Japan is an example of this form of monoculturalism. However, most recently, the success of several high-profile Japanese people of mixed heritage has raised questions about perceptions that the Japanese society is homogeneous. The key high-profile examples we would like to highlight are the number of foreigners in Japan's Rugby squad, the female tennis champion Naomi Osaka as well as Miss Japan Ariana Miyamoto. A recent trend that in our view is worth watching.

COMPANY DNA AND CULTURE

To add to this complexity, experienced D&I Leaders and CEOs will also have a keen eye on their company culture, cultural mix and historical growth. There is a certain risk of creating 'mono-cultures' at the top of the organization, ignoring the local cultural context and career progression. To give you an example, a large global French company with the majority of global headcount in France and its leaders coming through the ranks of the French education and internal promotions, might end up with French expatriates in leadership positions all around the world. The same obviously applies to large US multinationals with Americans calling the shots also outside of the US, Germans as the predominant leaders of large German multinationals etc. You get the picture. While this might be the natural and right approach during global expansion and under a growth scenario, we recommend a fair and equal approach to promoting local talent, once the Group has reached a certain maturity. If this dynamic is left alone and overlooked for too long, talent will be frustrated and leave and with it, the opportunity to create a truly inclusive global organization.

CONCLUSION AND RECOMMENDATIONS

These data from Europe, Switzerland and Japan, show that the US approach to Race & Ethnicity will not work or apply elsewhere and anywhere. However, we continue to see the reflex of D&I Leaders and CEOs to base their Race & Ethnicity strategy on the US model. This leads to misunderstandings, misinterpretations and deep frustrations. We recommend a more holistic view, respecting the internal company DNA and a very, very local approach to a 'global' Race & Ethnicity strategy. For a Swiss company for example, progress in Race & Ethnicity will be achieved by a higher representation of Italians at senior levels, whereas in Japan, the best cultural pace might be a growing number of employees being from a mixed heritage background and finally the promotion of local talent, if all your expats are from France.

'SELF-IDENTIFICATION' AND ROBUST COMPANY DATA?

Typically, every sound D&I strategy is based on state-of-the-art analytics. This is an easy step when it comes to Gender Equality or Age Diversity. Collecting robust and meaningful data for representation of LGBTQ+, Disability or Race & Ethnicity is incredibly hard, it may even be impossible.

Recently, the most common and evolving approach we have noticed, is the so called 'Self-identification'. Self-identification is when an employee discloses their diversity identity to their employer, including Race & Ethnicity, LGBTQ+, or Disability status. A Self-identification survey therefore allows employers to determine which employees self-identified as members of one or more of the "designated groups".

On the surface, Self-identification is an important tool that provides an avenue for employees to anonymously share their diversity data so that their employers can implement strategies to build a culture that supports all employees and measure their progress towards their diversity goals. While we appreciate the value of such surveys, we would like to pose some provocative questions, before you run ahead in your organization:

- Will you make your survey mandatory or voluntary for all?
- What is your baseline percentage of responses for meaningful results?
- What *additional* information that you don't already have, will you gain?
- What is your commitment to act and follow-up regarding representation?
- How will you combine your equal pay data with the results from the survey?
- How specific and locally relevant will your survey be?

- Who, how and what will be communicated after the survey?

Only, and only if you and your leadership team have carefully considered all the above, would we recommend a companywide survey asking employees to self-identify.

RACE & ETHNICITY ERG - SETTING YOU UP FOR SUCCESS

We can hardly think of a more impactful space for an ERG than in the field of Race & Ethnicity. A successful ERG will aim to inspire and support your minority ethnic colleagues and their allies to perform to their best abilities in an open, inclusive and supportive environment. The ERG works together with your senior leaders and HR to engage and influence the company's policy and culture from the top down, offering guidance and education to address different ethnicity stereotypes that affect your colleagues. Through activities and events your ERG also supports the professional development of its members, providing them with mentoring and career development opportunities. Ideally, your ERG will partner with the business to embed ethnicity initiatives to promote Inclusion.

QUICK SUMMARY: RACE & ETHNICITY

- Race and ethnicity are not the same. Race is a social construct that has historically been used to classify human beings according to physical or biological characteristics. Ethnicity is something a person acquires or ascribes to and refers to a shared culture, such as language, practices, and beliefs
- The complexities are vast and very much depend on where your organization operates
- Europe is increasingly a region marked by cultural diversity and foreign-born populations. In addition, being black in the EU often means racism and poor jobs, as black people in the EU face unacceptable difficulties in getting a decent job because of their skin color.

XVII. PEOPLE WITH DISABILITY

"The difference between the right word and the almost-right word is the difference between lightning and a lightning bug".
- Mark Twain.

It might be a shocking reveal right from the start, however, we have probably spent more time in our D&I careers debating the right terminology for Disability, than in any other dimension of D&I. And we admit that this deterred focus is awfully wrong. Hence, we might learn as much as you from this chapter.

When it comes to the terminology, this is the list and it might not be exhaustive: Disability, People with different abilities, people with special needs, differently abled, physically challenged, people with health conditions and impairments.

We understand that using the term *Disability* is widely accepted and less offensive or overly construed as some of the above. The tone in your strategy comes from the positive, i.e., improved physical accessibility, support and access to jobs.

What types of Disability might we expect to see in the workplace?

We will find four broad categories of Disability in the workplace: 1) Intellectual 2) Physical 3) Sensory and 4) Mental Illness.

These are further categorized in eight sub-categories:

1. Mobility and Physical Impairments
2. Spinal Cord Disabilities
3. Head injuries – Brain Disability
4. Vision Disability
5. Hearing Disability
6. Cognitive and Learning Disabilities
7. Psychological Disorders
8. Invisible Disabilities

16% of the world's population, or 1.2bn people are persons with disabilities.

On this note, did you know that in many countries there is a quota for hiring people with Disabilities? Quota systems for private and/or public enterprises or institutions exist in most countries in Europe. Their target is to stimulate labor demand by committing employers to employ a certain share of employees with disabilities. Typically, the stipulated share ranges between 2% and 7% of the workforce. In most countries the degree of fulfilment ranges between 30% and 70%. According to available empirical data, quota systems only lead to small net employment gains. While already employed persons who become disabled and can be included are more likely to remain employed, quotas only provide small incentives to hire disabled people. Sadly, we have seen a number of cases during our career, where organizations quietly went down the route of paying the very small penalty and by doing so avoiding the quota all together. We recommend a state-of-the-art-strategy as follows:

YOUR INCLUSIVE DISABILITY STRATEGY

Closely consult and actively involve persons with Disabilities and their representative organizations (for example ERGs) in everything you do; ensuring full accessibility for all to your company's buildings and facilities, workspaces, information and communications, conferences and events – with specific measures equipment and services to achieve it.

Think about it, if you manage to implement and execute all elements of this strategy, your company will be in the top tier 0.1% of organizations globally.

TALENT ATTRACTION AND ON-BOARDING

Given the unique challenges and opportunities of hiring and on-boarding, your recruitment strategy deserves a deeper look. Let's say you and your senior leadership team have committed to hiring candidates that fall under one of the eight sub-categories of Disability above. Where and how do you even start? Posting tailored job ads specifically addressing the topic of Disability? How? Which one? Where? This will inevitably fail.

We recommend two ways of attracting more diverse talent to your organization: a) reach out to your local NGOs and specific organizations in this field, as they will typically have a strong network or even an active candidate base of job seekers and, b) instead of targeting a specific segment, make your whole hiring process more inclusive, by using the appropriate tools and language in your job ads and training your recruiters and hiring managers accordingly. Here accessibility for example expands to considering advertising for the hearing and vision impaired candidates. In addition, promote your inclusive culture on your company website and by doing so, reduce hurdles to apply.

Special attention, care, awareness and consideration has to be brought to the on-boarding process. We have seen too many teams not up for this challenge and opportunity. Again, we recommend that you openly discuss with the candidate, what they need for a smooth transition into their new role, whether it is in special equipment, access or understanding. Luckily, we have also seen many times, how adding Diversity will allow the whole team to perform at a higher level given that standard work processes are reviewed and improved to fit all.

ON THE SPECTRUM – NEURODIVERSITY

Harvard University describes Neurodiversity as the idea that people experience and interact with the world around them in many ways; there is no one 'right' way of thinking, learning, and behaving, and differences are not viewed as deficits.

The word Neurodiversity refers to the Diversity of all people, but it is often used in the context of autism spectrum disorder (ASD), as well as other neurological or developmental conditions such as ADHAD or learning disabilities.

How can employers make their workplace more Neurodiversity-friendly? Here are the official recommendations:

- Offer small adjustments to an employee's workspace to accommodate any sensory needs, such as:
    - Sound sensitivity: offer a quiet break space, communicate expected loud noises (like fire drills), offer noise-cancelling headphones
    - Movements: allow the use of fidget toys, allow extra movement breaks, offer flexible seating

- Use a clear communication style:
    - Avoid sarcasm, euphemisms, and implied messages
    - Provide concise verbal and written instructions for tasks and break tasks down into small steps

- Inform people about workplace / social etiquette, and don't assume someone deliberately breaking the rules or being rude
- Try to give advance notice if plans are changing, and provide a reason for the change
- Don't make assumptions – ask a person's individual preferences, needs, and goals
- Be kind, be patient

Did you notice something? Exactly, isn't this how all of us would like to be treated? A perfect example, why this enhanced attention to detail and human care will benefit anyone. We hear this a lot!

QUICK SUMMARY: PERSONS WITH DISABILITIES

- Person's disabilities include those who have long-term physical, mental, intellectual, or sensory impairments which in interaction with various barriers may hinder their full and effective participation in the workplace
- People with disabilities make up an estimated one billion, or 15 % of the world's population. About 80 % are of working age. The right of people with disabilities to decent work, however, is frequently denied. People with disabilities, particularly women with disabilities, face enormous attitudinal, physical, and informational barriers to equal opportunities in the world of work
- To be successful in sourcing and acquiring talent with disabilities, it is important to successfully prepare your recruiters and future employees. Measures employers are implementing range from (physical) accessibility to active inclusion within the team.

XVIII. CEO LEADERSHIP

Nothing good will happen, literally nothing... without the leadership of the organization fully on board. Thinking that D&I will happen 'by itself' or is merely 'a matter of time', is both naïve and wishful thinking. D&I requires a clear strategy, a substantial budget, a brave and capable D&I Leader and their team AND full alignment with the CEO and the leadership team.

The most effective organizational structure for driving diversity and inclusion in an organization is one that involves all levels of the organization, from the CEO to the employees. A successful diversity and inclusion strategy must have the backing of the executive team, including the CEO, and must involve all employees in the organization. Furthermore, ERGs can play an important role in promoting diversity and inclusion by serving as a supportive community for underrepresented groups and a channel for their voices to be heard.

The CEO should set goals and targets, create policies, and provide the necessary resources and support to achieve these goals by setting an example and demonstrating a commitment to D&I. The leadership team should also be held accountable for meeting these objectives and should report on their progress on a regular basis.

Employees are the foundation of any organization, and their participation is essential to the success of any diversity and inclusion initiative. Employee engagement can be achieved through a variety of methods, including regular trainings and workshops, regular communication about the importance of diversity and inclusion, and the creation of opportunities for employees to share their experiences and perspectives.

Luckily, more and more CEOs have become very skilled and vocal on D&I matters and are openly sharing such support with their employees and via social media. It is no surprise that these are the organizations where we have seen most of the progress. A strong message from the CEO and her leadership team will go a long way. Yes, it is true that D&I can be an unfamiliar and challenging topic with its many complexities, but herein lies the opportunities to have real impact and to make change happen. We recommend staying curious and well informed.

The risk of getting D&I wrong should not be taken lightly. If your organization doesn't have real leadership for Diversity & Inclusion, your employees might become disengaged, they might sue you for discrimination at work, your reputation might suffer, and you could miss opportunities to launch new products.

On the other hand, if you run your organization well, it will become truly irresistible.

QUICK SUMMARY: CEO LEADERSHIP

- Diversity, Equity, and Inclusion have taken a center stage on many corporate agendas. This has largely been driven by increased social justice pressure from investors, boards, media and society. It is important to remember that diversifying the workforce is not only the right thing to do, but it also makes good business sense
- In this book, supported by ample research, we have shown that focusing on D&I, leads to increased innovation, better business outcomes and increased workplace effectiveness
- Increasingly, CEOs are implementing their D&I strategy like any other business strategy. The same internal tracking mechanism is applied. It is equally important to communicate openly and authentically about progress vs goals internally and externally.

XIX. EMPLOYEE RESOURCE GROUPS (ERGs)

There has been a significant evolution and growth of Employee Resource Groups (ERGs) over the last 30 years. First, the name has changed. Once called simply networks or affinity groups, they are in today's world referred to as not only ERGs, but also Business Resource Groups. The name significantly moved away from their original goals of supporting Diversity & Inclusion to being broader and more business focused. As the name transformed, the number of ERGs also is on the rise. More companies are adding ERGs, and those that have them already are creating more groups.

Advanced organizations with a well-designed Diversity & Inclusion strategy will have at least these ERGs in place and fully equipped with a budget and clearly defined roles and responsibilities: an ERG to foster the professional development of women, an ERG to promote LGBTQ+ Inclusion, the ERG reflecting the different generations in the workplace, and an ERG on Race & Ethnicity. ERGs around Wellness and Wellbeing are less likely, while ERGs looking into Mental Health are on the rise and so are ERGs working on the topic of Disability.

Now, what exactly do we mean, when we highlight the business focus? Successful ERGs will add to the bottom line of the organization. Examples can be found by innovation or product design and related ideas directly coming from members of the ERGs, or indirectly by an external representation of the organization through the ERG in (social) media.

Internally ERGs are a key partner and stakeholder of the D&I Leader, the Leadership Team and a valuable resource and sounding board for the Diversity & Inclusion Advisory Council. Well-functioning ERGs will be allowed and equipped to speak up and share directly and unfiltered the 'pulse of the organization'. We therefore strongly recommend considering moving the budget for the ERG under Business Strategy, Business Development or the CEO Office. The work as a member or leader of an ERG will be time consuming and, in most cases, voluntary and on top of the day job. In addition, ERGs are increasingly becoming regional or global. Therefore, it is vital to have a robust ERG structure in place to start with. Given the nature of ERG work, we recommend sharing responsibilities at the top by appointing a Chair and a Co-Chair. Employees in these roles will drive the ERG strategy, communication, events and presentations. To avoid burnout or fatigue and to give other employees an opportunity to lead the ERG, these roles should typically rotate after two years.

Roles and responsibilities will need to be clearly defined and agreed with other stakeholders, namely the D&I Lead, HR and the Leadership. Here it is worth mentioning that the Leadership (CEO) together with D&I remains the single owner of design and implementation of the overall D&I strategy. While the ERG is a valuable source of information and knowledge, its role is distinctly different from the other stakeholders mentioned. To avoid confusion or conflict, we recommend to clearly map out the purpose and role of the ERG in writing at the outset.

QUICK SUMMARY: EMPLOYEE RESOURCE GROUPS (ERGs)

- Why are they called 'Resource Groups'? ERGs have historically been diversity and inclusion networks that allowed professionals to connect. ERGs, originally called workplace affinity groups, began in the 1960s in response to racial tensions in the United States. Nowadays, ERGs are powerful resources for facilitating discussions and providing networks for professionals based on shared identities, experiences and allyship
- In the past few decades, companies have expanded ERG topics and begun implementing chapters worldwide, and today, ERGs are integrated into business strategies as imperatives. Top ranked companies will have ERGs
- Wherever D&I sits within your organization, we recommend an independent ERG budget sitting within your Corporate Strategy department or similar.

XX. KEY STAKEHOLDERS

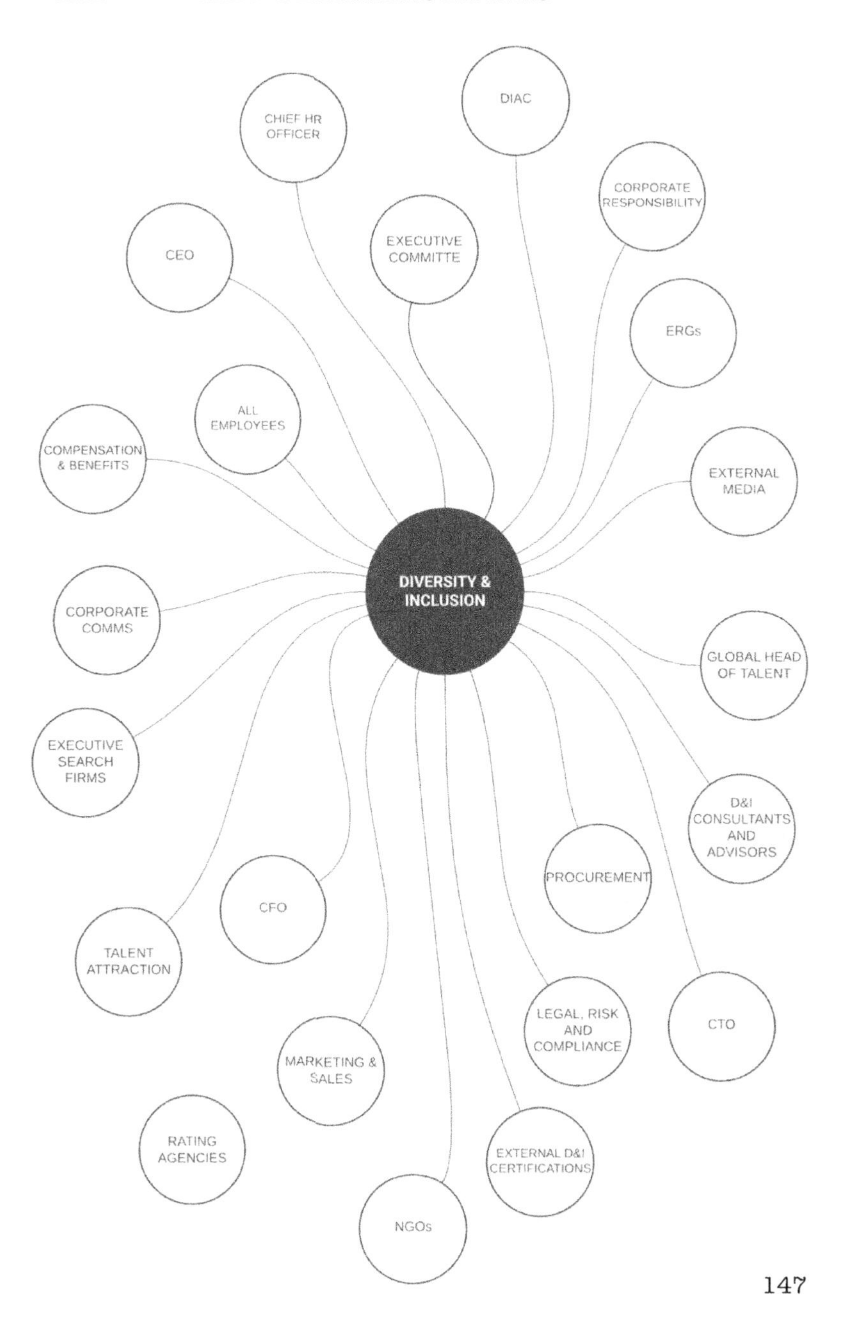

If we were to picture a typical Mind Map with 'Diversity & Inclusion' in the middle as the main bubble, there would be a myriad of connectors branching out. Let's take a closer look.

Diversity & Inclusion collaborates with:

CEO

Arguably, the most important stakeholder to engage. Positive change starts at the top. We believe for D&I to have impact, a dotted line into the CEO and strong alignment with an open and constructive two-way-communication is critical. We ran the data, modern and highly successful organizations are led by leaders, who understand, challenge and appreciate the value of Diversity & Inclusion.

CHIEF HR OFFICER

The Chief HR Officer will be your most important partner. Together you can move mountains, provided you share the same vision. He or she will navigate and orchestrate the role of Diversity & Inclusion vis-à-vis the other direct reports of his / her team. This will inevitably require some tough calls and – as Diversity & Inclusion goes across all dimensions with the Human Resources function – the D&I leader needs to be a true team player in return.

ALL EMPLOYEES

A diverse and inclusive workplace benefits everyone. We recommend starting with a strong foundation by anchoring Diversity & Inclusion within the workforce. It is important to understand the specific D&I needs and expectations of the employees. Focus groups, informal and formal channels like the intranet and surveys will give you a well-rounded picture and a plan to start with. Don't forget that information and expectation must flow both ways. It is equally important to keep employees informed about your D&I strategy, key milestones and your specific commitment.

EXECUTIVE COMMITTEE

Ideally the CEO and CHRO will support the D&I strategy, however, strong D&I leadership is required in bringing the entire Executive Committee along. D&I leaders need to understand the business and familiarize themselves with the key KPIs the organization has in place, in particular financial data. The question to ask: How can D&I enable and support the business leaders in reaching their goals.

DIVERSITY & INCLUSION ADVISORY COUNCIL

We strongly recommend a Diversity & Inclusion Advisory Council or D&I Board. This council consists of selected members of the Executive Committee, the CEO, CHRO and the D&I leader. The Diversity & Inclusion Advisory Council meets regularly to agree on the D&I strategy, how best to execute various initiatives, approve budget and define the vision & roadmap and its oversight.

EMPLOYEE RESOURCE GROUPS (ERGS)

While the D&I team serves all employees, members of the ERGs come together in formal networks to invest time, resources and energy on one of the D&I dimensions. ERGs are a crucial partner for the success and credibility of Diversity & Inclusion. While they act independently from D&I - we strongly suggest a separate budget – both the ERGs and D&I are working towards common goals and in our experience a lot of effort needs to be invested into making this relationship work and to 'speak with one voice'. Given the increasing role ERGs play within companies, we have dedicated a separate chapter outlining in more detail the dos and don'ts that come to mind.

GLOBAL HEAD OF TALENT

Diversity & Inclusion as a strong link to career development and succession planning. Throughout our career we have seen the biggest impact on moving the needle by collaborating with a strong Head of Talent, who ensures that D&I is a key component of any Talent Review and data on gender, age, race and sexual orientation are considered when looking at the successor pool. Data, data, data... good D&I starts with a deep data analysis and when it comes to hiring, promotions and exits, these are tracked by the Global Head of Talent.

COMPENSATION & BENEFITS

This very valuable relationship is too often overlooked. Aligning with the Global Head of Compensation & Benefits can, in our experience reap the most amazing results. Examples are: Equal Pay, Family Leave and any other Leave, New Ways of Working and its related policies to workplace and working hours and days. In addition, D&I is at consideration when it comes to Global Mobility and collaboration and will go a long way on top of being highly appreciated by employees.

TALENT ATTRACTION

D&I isn't limited to existing employees and always aims at the external talent pipeline. The colleagues from Talent Attraction play a key role in ensuring that their process to attract talent is inclusive; starting from how job adverts and job descriptions are worded to ensure inclusive language, to running an interview process that is sensitive to candidate's needs. They are the gatekeepers to ensure that there is a balanced slate of candidates being reviewed and assessed by an equally balanced interview panel.

CFO

Yes, as any other business function, D&I will cost money and resources. On the other hand, there will be gains produced in return. As Human Resources as a whole, D&I operates in the space of living assets vs. fixed assets. Once this is mutually understood and appreciated, investment into D&I can be offset for example by reducing office space and consequently cancelling of lease agreements in the context of New Ways of Working. Equally a successful and attractive Family Leave Policy will do so much to attract and retain talent, that a specific Dollar amount can be put against the initial investment. This requires D&I leaders to be highly familiar with the numbers.

CTO

Increasingly D&I sips over into IT initiatives and the COVID pandemic has accelerated this collaboration. Tools like MS Teams, Zoom, Slack etc. – who are owned and run by the IT department – impact D&I daily. Whether it is to jointly announce the introduction of all meetings by default being set as remote meetings, or the same message on a healthy relationship to being online vs focus time, these are just a few of examples where the IT department and D&I are working together. As D&I leader it is important to keep up to date with the most recent virtual tools and IT trends.

CORPORATE RESPONSIBILITY

Often, the D&I team alongside colleagues from Corporate Responsibility present during the same meeting to the same audience, this is how much these two functions are intertwined. Whether it is topics brought in the space of Human Rights, or relating to the ‘S’ in ESG, there is such a strong overlap of Corporate Responsibility / Corporate Sustainability that in some organizations they are brought under ‘one roof’.

CORPORATE COMMUNICATION

D&I success is not possible without Communication, Communication, Communication. And it is no surprise that good communication always requires repetition. We have seen firsthand, how both departments can benefit from each other in spreading the message internally and externally, of who, how, why leads the efforts of making the organization more inclusive and diverse internally as well as attracting external talent. This, of course, includes the first window to the external world, the company-wide external webpage. Our recommendation is not only a one-time-upload of the D&I agenda and strategy, but to earmark time in the corporate calendar for regular updates, as in our experience this obvious step too often gets lost.

MARKETING & SALES

Of course, it goes a long way when you have products and services that speak to an inclusive audience and consumer base! You will find many examples in this book and by simply looking around you. Working together with Marketing & Sales is not only usually great fun, but it also adds to the business relevance of what we do. And to mention something which equally applies to the CFO and the CTO: these functions typically lend themselves to have a more strategic and robust female talent planning pipeline.

RISK, LEGAL & COMPLIANCE

The most common point for collaboration typically is the Code of Conduct or Code of Ethics the organization operates with. These will include the mention of Diversity, Equity, and Inclusion by clearly stating the areas concerned, i.e., Gender Equality, Gender Identity, Race & Ethnicity, Age and Disability. Furthermore, your organization might have a whistleblowing function in place, which will directly lead to involving D&I as far as discrimination, bullying and/or harassment is concerned. D&I became increasingly relevant for the Chief Risk Officer. In 2021 the first global ISO standard **#30415:2021 Human Resources management, Diversity and Inclusion** was released to give guidance on D&I for organizations around the globe.

PROCUREMENT

In addition to the obvious connection with Procurement as a D&I budget owner, supplier diversity plays an ever-increasing important role. We encourage a rather simple tracking system that allows quarterly reporting on the Diversity of suppliers. Keeping track of external suppliers who are themselves stating their commitment to D&I and of which category, goes a long way when such a report to the Board is required.

EXTERNAL MEDIA

Diversity & Inclusion lends itself to positive media coverage via external media partners like newspapers, podcasts, social media, and TV shows. Provided the story is authentic and credible, this is the best way to control the narrative. Endless CEOs and business leaders have started communicating externally on D&I with great success. Equally, we would like to highlight the position no company wants to be in: a negative media backlash due to lack of sensitivity for Diversity & Inclusion.

D&I CONSULTANTS & ADVISORS

As any other business function within the organization, D&I is no exception as the D&I leader and her team will contract with a number of external D&I consultants and advisors. Unless the team works with long standing partners, a sound due diligence is recommended. D&I can be a highly sensitive topic and small nuances in representation and wording will make a difference. In other words, before rolling out a worldwide D&I initiative with an external partner, run a few pilots to ensure everyone is aligned.

EXECUTIVE SEARCH FIRMS

Nine out of ten briefings which go out to Executive Search Firms today will include the following caveat: we are looking to hire a diversity candidate! For the client and search firm it is important to clarify from the beginning, how 'serious' this requirement is. Mostly it is! Therefore, it is frustrating for both parties and slows down the process if the long list or short list doesn't reflect the desired diverse candidate base. In our experience it doesn't pay off to invest into 'external female talent mapping' or similar projects. Mostly the client ends up paying a large sum for a list of potential candidates, but there's no successful role-fit-timing-ration. On the other hand, the conscious decision to hire a diversity candidate externally for a specific role has led to amazing recruitments.

EXTERNAL D&I CERTIFICATIONS AND LABELS

Whether it is Equal Pay, the LGBT+ community or the Human Rights Index, there are a growing number of external certifications and labels for the organization to consider. Some are very broad in nature, like Top Employer, some are very specific as the Workplace Equality Indices by Stonewall. If and when you are ready, we advise to work with external certifications and labels to track your progress, address potential gaps of your D&I strategy and to acquire external validation in order to communicate.

NGOs

Wherever you operate, there will be plenty of NGOs around you fostering Diversity & Inclusion. Make them your valuable partner. In their given space, the NGO will be happy to provide valuable data and insights and they come with high credibility. In our experience, this external partnership is too often overlooked, as working with NGOs, and implementing their wisdom and approach into your

D&I strategy, requires more of your resources than working with specialized consultants. Here it is worth to walk the extra mile.

RATING AGENCIES

Do investors actually care about Diversity? Numerous studies and analyst reports find the answer is Yes. For listed U.S. companies, a study found that racial and ethnic diversity on the corporate boards of large caps had a significant positive impact on the stock price. Generally speaking, higher diversity numbers in any dimension translates into higher stock prices. It gets better, if a company's diversity numbers beat those of the industry leader, the bump in stock price is even stronger. We predict that rating agencies like Standard & Poor's (S&P), Moody's and Fitch will open up on Diversity. On February 11, 2022, Bloomberg Law posted that most of S&P 500 companies mentioned Diversity in annual reports. Large publicly traded companies around the world are ramping up Diversity & Inclusion disclosures discussing work to achieve equitable businesses in annual reports.

To firmly anchor Diversity & Inclusion within your organization, you will want to have the right structure in place to effectively collaborate with the numerous stakeholders mentioned here.

XXI. AVOIDING BACKLASH

Now that we have explored the dimensions of Diversity & Inclusion, it is time to address the topic of backlash. Whether you are a CDO (Chief Diversity & Inclusion Officer) or CEO/Chief HR Officer, it's essential to be aware of the potential backlash you may face and to be prepared to address it. Our operating model, when applied consistently, will be a great resource for lasting success.

One key strategy for avoiding backlash is to think global and act local. This means considering the big picture of diversity and inclusion issues while also paying attention to the specific needs and concerns of your local community. By taking a nuanced approach to diversity and inclusion, you can ensure that your efforts are effective and well-received.

Another important skill to cultivate as a diversity and inclusion leader is to act like a polymath. This means being able to think broadly and creatively about solutions to complex problems. By drawing on a diverse range of skills and perspectives, you can develop innovative approaches to diversity and inclusion that address the unique needs of your organization.

It's also essential to recognize the importance of both top-down and bottom-up approaches to diversity and inclusion. While leadership plays a crucial role in setting the tone and priorities for diversity and inclusion efforts, it's also essential to engage and empower employees at all levels of the organization. By creating a culture of inclusion and collaboration, you can ensure that everyone feels valued and supported.

Staying in touch with the zeitgeist is another key strategy for avoiding backlash in the field of diversity and inclusion. This means paying attention to the cultural, social, and political trends that shape our world and adapting your approach accordingly. By staying attuned to the needs and concerns of your community, you can ensure that your diversity and inclusion efforts are relevant and responsive.

Finally, data is critical for analyzing the effectiveness of your diversity and inclusion efforts and communicating their impact to stakeholders. By collecting and analyzing data, you can identify areas of strength and weakness in your approach and make evidence-based decisions about how to move forward. As the saying goes, what gets measured gets done, so it's essential to prioritize data collection and analysis.

Taken together, these strategies form the basis of our proven DEI operating model that can help you avoid or anticipate backlash in the field of diversity and inclusion. By thinking globally and acting locally, acting like a polymath, embracing both top-down and bottom-up approaches, staying in touch with the zeitgeist, and prioritizing data collection and analysis, you can create a culture of inclusion and belonging benefitting everyone in your organization.

With more than 50 years of practical D&I experience, this model has been tested and refined over time, making it a reliable framework for achieving lasting success in the field of diversity and inclusion.

QUICK SUMMARY: AVOIDING BACKLASH

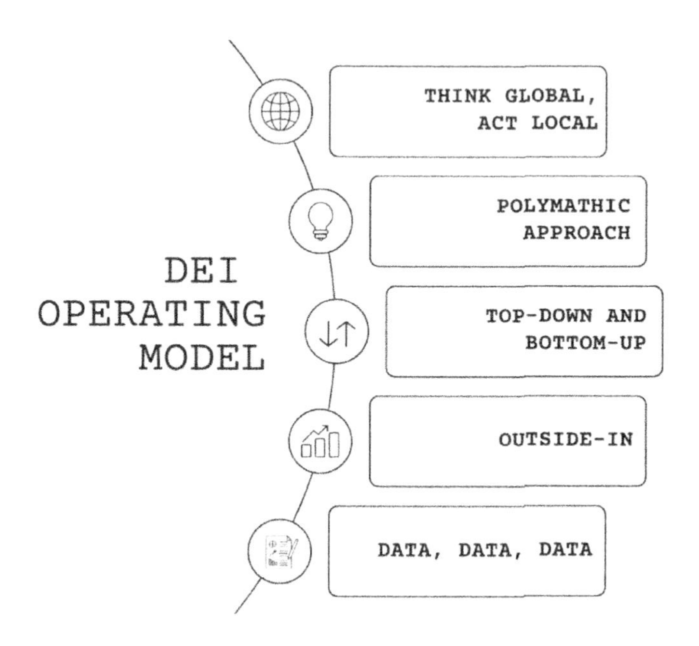

RESOURCES

The third chapter of the book provides readers with a wealth of resources related to D&I:

- Including Inclusive Leaves, Supplier Diversity and Marketing & Innovation and Branding
- Additionally, readers will learn how to implement and run a successful Executive Sponsorship Program, a key strategy for promoting diversity & inclusion in the workplace
- Finally, the chapter provides a comprehensive overview of Organizational Network Analytics (ONA), which in our experience is the best technology for measuring inclusion in organizations, given readers the tools they need to ensure their efforts are successful and impactful.

XXII. INCLUSIVE LEAVES

As we have said it many times before, when it comes to a successfully deployed D&I strategy, talking the talk is not enough, trainings alone – in particular unconscious bias trainings are not enough, and changing people's minds and behaviours needs to be supported by changes directly in the system: the procedures and policies that make up this so called system a corporation.

Part of these fundamentals that make up the structure of a corporation are the employee benefits and the paid and unpaid leaves. These leaves can make or break the employer brand of your organization and as we have seen lately, they become the main features of the job descriptions when looking for a new job. Recruiters are smart enough to use them as the main USPs of a job offer, flaunting them like a new designer dress in front of the candidates' eyes.

As you might know, there are many types of leave and below we decided to focus on the ones that will bring you the biggest "bang for the buck".

FAMILY LEAVE

In this section, we are going to set the bar high for you. We are the creators of the number 1 most inclusive family leave policy in the corporate world, to date. A truly international policy, valid in more than 60 locations. Regardless, if the location is a developing or an advanced society country, in both extremes the policy brought incremental changes. Regardless if someone works in an office, on the field or in a factory. Regardless of the nature of becoming a parent - surrogacy, adoption or natural birth, even where the local environment doesn't fully support all options. Regardless of the gender of the parent, everyone gets minimum 20 week of paid leave to take care of their new family members. And all of that at 100% pay.

But this is just to set the tone and the expectations. Read along and we will get you there.

Taking the gender out of the family leave. Seriously, in 2023, we will not be pledging the case that some genders are more suitable to be parents - all of them can be great at it, and all of them can be terrible at it. For the fight of gender equality and closing the gap, an equal and inclusive family leave has a great impact. For example, in the typical binary gender split studies, we have seen that when men take parental leave, everybody benefits. Studies show a woman's earnings rise about 6.7% for every month of paternity leave taken by her partner.
Beyond the pay gap, inclusive family leaves can help foster co-parenting and deconstruct traditional and harmful gender norms which are typically seen in households. And last but not least, when the time comes to decide who gets the new job and the promotion - Shangela or Buck, nobody can disqualify Shangela anymore because of her potentially becoming a mother and going away. The same suspicion should and will apply to Buck, who has an equal probability that he will become a parent and go away on a leave to take care of his new family member.

Firstly, let's settle on the terminology. It began with maternity leave – and still in most countries of the world is the only type of family leave available. One could say, by the time women were started to be generally accepted in the workplace, men found yet another mechanism to keep them at home with assigning them the duties of taking care of their newborns, as it just comes more "naturally" to women to be parents. It is tricky to evaluate, as on one side it appears as if women who became parents are being protected by the law, while on the other side, the fight for equality in the workforce continues to grow. Once the Scandinavians in 1993 realized fathers can also make great parents and caregivers, the first paternity leave was introduced in the world. And like this, we immediately arrive at the first point of the inclusive family leave – Do Not Differentiate between maternity and paternity leave. By using the term Family Leave you are going to be inclusive of all kinds of parents, all genders. Anyone can become a parent, period.

Secondly, driven by the first rule, is the quantitative benefit you will decide to provide to your employees. The number of weeks you provide the benefit for, can have quite a broad range, but the golden rule is to not differentiate - yet again -based on the gender. And this will not come easy as if you look elsewhere, many organizations claim to have a modern and equal family leave, then when you look into the details, they typically provide 4 weeks for the fathers, and a significantly larger number for the mothers. Where does that lead us? Back to square one. This is a battle that you cannot give up, as it's the strongest selling point of your policy. And, for extra points with your employees – current or future ones, land on a number that goes beyond what the local government is offering. At the end of the day, the business sector is there to inspire the state to do better and push the boundaries of society.

Thirdly, who counts as an eligible parent for your family leave benefit? Short answer, everyone. Long answer, any employee that becomes a parent via natural birth, via adoption or via surrogacy. In fact, the important notion here is to motivate and support especially the non-typical parent suspects to have the courage to actually take the leave. It is not enough to just offer a benefit if it's a benefit that nobody dares to use. These examples need to be set across the organizations but especially at the top.

Fourthly, data and reporting. Without any doubt if the policy is designed based on our principles, it will be successful. But your CFO will need to be convinced with some numbers as there is a bit of math involved. Probability scenarios and replacement costs calculations will be helpful in this case. And the replacement costs can easily be solved as you will not need to replace your employees in the managerial and above ranks – these open slots can be turned into an opportunity for other colleagues to take more responsibilities and expand their skillset. Define KPIs like the gender split, the eligible employees, the take-up rate and particularly the utilization rate. Not the same thing and both are important as we need to know not only how many people decided to take family leave, but did they utilize 100% of their given benefit.

Lastly, an extra tip: think about going beyond and start drawing outside of the box. What is a modern family in 2022? Could you offer benefits for surrogacy, in vitro procedures, adaptation, loss of a child etc. Any direction towards this kind of mindset is a win-win situation.

TRANSITIONING POLICY

As the world continues to evolve and progress, so does our understanding of gender fluidity, identity and expression. In order to ensure a safe and welcoming workplace for all employees, it is important to have an established gender transitioning policy in place. Having clear guidelines and expectations can help to create a supportive environment and ensure that all employees are respected. To be very blunt from the start, for this policy, the focus is not on the "leave" part, as the leave is in most instances covered by the health insurance, but the focus is on the supporting systems and individuals around the person who is transitioning, to make sure the journey is as smooth as possible.

Establishing a gender transitioning policy at work can be a complex and daunting task. It requires a deep understanding of gender identity, knowledge of local and state laws, and an ability to communicate effectively with colleagues and employees. Creating a gender transitioning policy can help protect everyone in the workplace, create an inclusive and safe environment, and ensure that all employees are treated fairly and with respect. With the right guidance and information, it's possible to develop a gender transitioning policy that not only meets legal requirements, but also serves the needs of all employees. This article will provide an overview of the key steps for creating a gender transitioning policy at work.

Here we will also cover some of the basics. To begin with, what is the term transitioning? The term transitioning signifies the process and/or steps that an individual goes through, in order to live in the gender, they identify as. Most people will immediately jump into the assumption that every trans person undertakes a medical intervention. And it cannot be further from the truth. Each person's transitioning journey is unique, with no right or wrong way or a predetermined duration of the transitioning process. To date, the numbers show that around 42% of individuals don't dare to transition as they are afraid of losing their job. So, it is even more important to proactively create supporting mechanism and to involve the concerned individuals in the creation of those mechanism.

There are four areas to consider when creating a transitioning policy:

Number one: disclosure. Without any discussions, it is up to the concerned person to decide if, when, how and to whom they need to announce their transition or to come out.

Administrative support – the least you can you. This is the area where organizations can be of great help. Imagine the numerous times a transitioning person had to deal with name changes, pronouns changes, countless hours spent filling in forms and waiting at the counter having to justify their transitioning. Most, we repeat, most of the records within your organization can be easily changed to reflect the person's preferred data. Except for some official payroll records, be proactive in taking care of this aspect that will be highly appreciated and impactful.

Managerial guide: Managers and senior leaders play a major role in ensuring your employees who are transitioning have the right support in place. You could be in a position where you are the manager of a trans or transitioning employee or a candidate, or your own manager might be going through the process. Via this guide, managers will learn how to support their employees in the best way possible: developing and creating a plan, safeguard them from other colleagues and teammates, stakeholders list in terms of who are the people they might need to contact during the process, address names, pronouns, how to make sure their careers are intact and any other considerations relevant in the situation.

Indeed, creating a gender transitioning policy can be an intimidating and complex task, but with the right information and resources, it can save human lives.

SABBATICAL LEAVE

If your business is looking to add a sabbatical leave policy to its list of employee benefits, you'll be joining a growing number of companies who understand the importance of taking a break. The world, particularly during and after Covid, has seen a tremendous increase in mental health challenges, as depression and anxiety cost the global economy 1 trillion dollars per year, according to the WHO. Let's start slowly by introducing what is the concept of the sabbatical leave and where does it come from historically, so we can end this section with advice on how to make the best of a sabbatical policy for your organization.

A sabbatical leave is an extended period of time away from work or school, providing an opportunity to travel, pursue a passion or take a break from the everyday grind. A period of extended time away from work, typically ranging anywhere from a few weeks up to a year, it gives the employees an opportunity to pursue personal or professional interests outside of their regular job duties. While the concept of sabbatical leave has roots dating back hundreds of years, it has become increasingly popular in recent decades as employers have come to recognize the benefits associated with allowing employees to take extended breaks from their jobs. The concept of sabbatical leave has its roots in religious tradition. In Judaism, for example, there is the concept of shmitah—a seven-year cycle during which all agricultural activities must be halted, and debts must be forgiven. Similarly, some Christian traditions observe something called sabbatical year—a year-long period during which all work must cease so that people can focus on spiritual renewal and contemplation.

It wasn't until the late 19th century that the concept of sabbatical leave began to gain traction among universities and other institutions of higher learning. As academic institutions sought ways to retain their best faculty members and encourage them to remain engaged and productive over long periods, they began offering extended leaves to provide faculty with an opportunity for personal growth and intellectual exploration. This eventually led to many private businesses adopting similar policies, making sabbaticals available to their most valued employees as well. Still, today only 4% of companies offer paid sabbatical leave and 14% of companies offer unpaid sabbatical leave.

If we dive deep into the benefits of a sabbatical leave, there are many. Creating a sabbatical leave policy can be a great way to promote inclusion and belonging in the workplace. In today's world, it's important to recognize that people have different needs and life circumstances. And giving employees the freedom to take a break and recharge can be a great way to show that you care and are willing to invest in them. Sabbatical leave can help employees feel a sense of inclusion and belonging within their workplace and give them a chance to recharge and come back with fresh, innovative ideas. What's more, it can be a great way to attract and retain talent. When employees return from their extended break refreshed and energized by new experiences and perspectives gained along the way – it's not just good for them; it's good for business too!

Here are some specific advantages that come with taking a sabbatical:

- Improved mental health: taking a break from work allows employees to reduce stress and increase a sense of wellbeing. This can lead to feeling refreshed and energized when returning to work after the sabbatical leave is over.

- Increased creativity: Taking time off gives the chance to explore new hobbies or explore interests outside of the regular work schedule. This can help spark creative ideas which can be beneficial both personally and professionally upon returning to work.
- Clarity on career goals: taking time away from a job gives an opportunity for self-reflection which can help employees gain clarity on what direction they want their career path to go in next.
- Succession: sabbaticals also provide employers with an opportunity for succession planning; if one employee takes a long-term break from work then another employee may be given the chance to step up into a higher role during their absence. This provides valuable experience for those who may be looking to move up within a company or an organization.

But how do you go about creating a sabbatical leave policy? Well, there are a few steps you should take to make sure it's successful. First, decide what kind of leave you'll offer, such as paid or unpaid. In our opinion, a combination of both is the sweet spot. Give your employees a choice. It can always be a combination of paid sabbatical leave for volunteering opportunities and unpaid leave for longer self-discovery trips – for example. Then, determine who is eligible and how much time they can take off. Again, the combination and a progressive framework will be the key.

Different generations have different needs and expectations. For example, if you have a strict policy where the benefit is granted only after 10 years in the company, you're screwed. Millennials and Gen Z are by default excluded and you won't live a long enough life to see a millennial staying in your company for 10 consecutive years. So, the solution is to offer a progressive leave starting from three years of seniority. The higher the seniority, the higher the paid or unpaid leave, simple. Finally, establish what kind of activities employees can pursue during their sabbatical. With a little bit of planning, you can create a sabbatical leave policy that's sure to make everyone in your workplace happier and more productive. The policy should be clear and easy to understand and should include details on how long the sabbatical can last and what the employee can expect when they return, such as additional support or training. Even if you're not able to offer paid sabbaticals, it's still a great way to show that you value your employees and want them to be successful. Investing in your employees is always a good idea — and with a sabbatical leave policy, you can do just that!

When it comes down to it one thing is certain: sabbaticals are here to stay! With clear expectations set forth prior to departure this type of extended break is beneficial not only for the employee but also the employer as well - leading not only lead to increased employee engagement & productivity but also improved mental health & overall wellbeing! So why not consider introducing a sabbatical leave? It just might be exactly what you need right now.

MENSTRUATION LEAVE

For too long, the conversation around menstruation has been hushed and uncomfortable—but it's time to bring this issue out into the open. Yes, there are people who menstruate, no big shock there. Despite the taboo nature of the topic, discussing menstruation in the workplace is an important step towards creating a more equitable work environment. One way to do this is by implementing a menstrual leave policy, which can provide employees with additional support during their periods. Let's explore why menstrual leave policies are beneficial for both employers and employees.

Menstrual leave is an employee policy that allows individuals to take a day or two off from work each month due to menstruation-related issues such as cramps, migraines, fatigue, or other symptoms often associated with premenstrual syndrome (PMS). The exact number of days allowed will vary depending on your company's policy, but typically one or two days are offered as time off. There are numerous benefits associated with implementing menstrual leave policies in the workplace. First and foremost, it gives employees more control over their health decisions. Allowing individuals to take time off when they need it most can help reduce stress and make them feel supported in their roles. This can lead to higher productivity levels since employees are not dealing with unnecessary distractions while on the job. Additionally, menstrual leave policies can help build morale among workers since they know there is an option for taking care of themselves if needed. Overall, implementing menstrual leave policies at work is a great way to create a more equitable and supportive working environment for all employees—regardless of gender identity or expression. Not only does it give people more control over their health decisions, but it also helps build morale amongst staff members and saves money on costs associated with paid sick days or other forms of absenteeism due to PMS-related symptoms. It's time for us all to start talking about menstruation openly and honestly so that we can create better workplaces for everyone involved!

MENOPAUSE LEAVE

Another taboo?!?

(I'm sure you realized part of working in the D&I space is destigmatizing all these taboos that are part of our daily lives anyhow. But isn't it so much fun?? ☺)

It's time to break the silence on menopause in the workplace. With the number of people experiencing menopause increasing, it's time to acknowledge the unique needs of these employees. Thankfully, some forward-thinking companies have already introduced a menopause leave policy, allowing their employees the time and space to manage their menopausal symptoms. This policy is a win-win: it helps the employee and it helps the employer, as studies show that results in improved productivity and job satisfaction. In fact, many are so appreciative of their employer's understanding of their needs that they even dub it "the menopause bonus"! What's more, this policy sends a strong message to all employees that their employer respects and values them. After all, it's something that many of your employees will eventually experience. With physical symptoms like hot flashes and night sweats, mental health issues like depression and anxiety, and even cognitive difficulties like memory loss and difficulty concentrating, it's clear that the menopause can have a huge impact on an employee's day-to-day work. A menopause leave policy could be as simple as allowing employees to take extra days off when needed or offering flexible working hours. It could also cover the costs of special menopause treatments, like hormone therapy. Whatever the policy looks like, it will show your employees that you care about their wellbeing. So, if you're an employer, it pays to consider introducing a menopause leave policy. It's a small step that can make a big difference.

CAREGIVERS LEAVE

Last but not least, caregivers leave. As many employers are realizing, caregivers need to be given the same rights as any other employee. That's why companies are beginning to implement a caregiver leave at work policy. This policy allows caregivers to take the necessary time off to take care of their loved ones without the fear of losing their job. Nearly 1 in 5 workers in the U.S. are also caregivers for ill, elderly or special-needs adults, according to Caregiving in the U.S., a 2020 AARP report. It's a win-win situation, as employers get to retain productive and motivated employees, while caregivers can take care of their families without sacrificing their careers. And while the policy is still in its infancy, more and more employers are recognizing the importance of a caregiver leave at work policy. Don't you want to be a trendsetter? It could be just the thing that your employees need to get the freedom to take care of their loved ones without worrying about the consequences.

QUICK SUMMARY: INCLUSIVE LEAVES

- Nowadays there are a number of Inclusive Leaves to consider: Family Leave, Sabbatical Leave, Bereavement Leave, Leave for Volunteering, Leave for Menstruation and Menopause, Disability Leave and Gender Transition Leave
- Traditionally, menopause and menstrual leave have been taboo topics. More recently though, an ever-increasing number of organizations have implemented both menopause and menstrual leave to eliminate the taboo and to recognize the physical and mental discomforts they can cause
- Enacting inclusive paid leave policies benefit both the employer and employee, as they help to attract and retain top talent. Prospective employees value workplaces that demonstrate a commitment to the health and wellbeing of all employees and their diverse families.

XXIII. EXECUTIVE SPONSORSHIP

'Women are *over-mentored* and *under-sponsored'*. That is the premise and starting point. At the early stages, we were all running in the same direction to get more women to the top: Mentoring, mentoring, mentoring was all the rage. But after more than 10 years of mentoring everywhere, we didn't see (any) results. If mentoring is 'to talk to someone', sponsoring is 'to talk *about* someone'. And that's what did the trick. As soon as we had senior leaders talking about Michelle, Amanda and Natalie in the famous moments of truth, one example being Talent Reviews, change started to happen. Ultimately, key decisions involve this human element.

THE PIE MODEL

Unfortunately, we are not talking about the tasty kind of PIE, but the kind of PIE that is really important to keep in mind when thinking about your career progression.

In 1996, Harvey Coleman explored the impact of PIE on the career success. Simply put, his work looks at three key elements that contribute to people progressing in their careers. He explains these three elements as:

1. **Performance** – how good are you at your job and how good the results are of what you do.
2. **Image** – is about you and how you are perceived. In the 1990s, the term 'personal brand' was even more used than it is today.

3. **Exposure** – is all about how well people know about what you do, i.e., not just your line manger but the level(s) above her too, as well as the leaders and partners of the other departments.

There is so much focus on technical skills and knowledge as we progress through education and indeed as we enter our first roles. However, as we move through our careers, those skills are simply expected, and it is about what else we can offer. This is particularly the case as there are fewer senior level jobs. Coleman asserts that, just 10% of career progression is down to performance. Yes, you read that right just 10%! That's why focusing on pure performance on technical skills and academics is often referred to as the 'entry ticket'.

This might sound very low but imagine the situation during a Talent Review where there are several candidates who are going for a promotion. They will have all been through interviewing to get the role in the first place and held onto their roles by providing their technical capabilities with the team. Therefore, that box is pretty much ticked. So, when the committee decides who gets promoted, they will assume the people being suggested performing well in their roles. This brings us onto the other 90%.

In this model, a gigantic 60% of career progression is based upon the Exposure element. So, when the committee hears your name being put forward, the individuals will search their minds for what they know about you, if anything. If they know nothing about you i.e., they have had no exposure to you then your chances of promotion are likely to be slim, your best outcome is probably a pay raise for good performance. Assuming they have had some exposure to you then this links into the final 30%, which is Image – what has been their perception when they interacted with you? Do they perceive you can take the next step and do well? What is their experience of you interacting with others?

Now you might ask, what does all this have to do with D&I in general and Gender Equality in particular? Well, guess what, women tend to spend their energy on the wrong 10%. The ExCom Sponsorship Program is here to elevate Exposure and Image and by doing so, making the Talent Review Process more equitable.

Key ingredients and set-up of a successful Executive Sponsorship Program

1. EXCOM SELECTION PROCESS

As a first step, each member of your Executive Team **chooses** one senior female talent for the duration of one year. Trust me, this will be the most challenging step. Allow for ample time and intellectual resources and convincing power for this step. Schedule a meeting with each individual member of your Executive Committee (ExCom). Provide them with enough background and information beforehand to have a meaningful discussion. And discuss with you they will want. You might be challenged with concerns like 'Sponsorship is like having a Protegee or Nepotism'. Yes and No is the answer. Men have risen to the top for centuries because they had Sponsors, were Protegees and Nepotism exists. Whether we like it, or not. In order for women to raise in the ranks, this is exactly what has been lacking.

Avoid matching members of your ExCom with senior female leaders. Let them choose. They choose who within the organization has the potential to sit at the table, make it to the boardroom. I once stumbled over the definition that the ideal Sponsor should be FAT and UGLY. FAT here equals in a 'position of power' and UGLY stands for someone, 'who is not afraid to speak up'. Makes total sense, doesn't it. In addition, the Sponsor put his or her leadership credibility and agency on the line to actively promote the **Sponsoree.** And, here we go, what a weird word. I spear you the time, don't try to find a better one. Protegee doesn't fly, at least not outside the US. Mentee is exactly not, what we are doing. Once the terminology has been used for some time, talking about Sponsorees will be widely accepted and get much easier.

Members of the ExCom cannot choose to sponsor one of their direct reports and ideally not within the same functional or geographical scope of their responsibilities. In my experience it helps tremendously to provide some further guidance. Top Female Talent means that the candidates for this program are seen as top talent as per the annual talent review, with an emphasis on their potential. As a broad guidance, we are talking about women, who have at least one or two career moves ahead of them, depending on where they sit in the organization.

2. INFORMING CANDIDATES

Once all ExCom members have made their choice and the women have been selected, the leader will inform his or her Sponsoree and share the good news. This might be the first time that the Female Leader hears not only about her selection, but also about the program as such, as it now concerns her. I recommend sharing a detailed written guide with both the Sponsor and the Sponsoree, tailored for their needs and most urgent questions.

3. KICK-OFF

The ideal kick-off event is held in person with all Sponsors and Sponsorees in the same room. This recommended approach is very powerful and sets up the program for success. This is an opportunity for everyone to 'get on the same page' regarding the program and its goals. As chaperone of the program, the D&I leader will repeat, how the program runs, for how long it lasts, map out the key dos and don'ts. Communication is repetition. Things like 'shadowing' might need further explanation and refinement. Questions about rhythm of meetings between Sponsor and Sponsoree will need to be addressed. The setting should allow for some formal and more relaxed interaction. For the women selected this is a once-in-a-career-opportunity. They will have exposure to the full ExCom and this opportunity shall be used wisely - as we learned from the PIE model.

4. CLOSURE AND LESSONS LEARNT, NEXT

The ExCom Sponsorship Program typically runs for one year. Make a point of carefully selecting individual feedback and room for improvement from all participants towards the end. In parallel, you will be busy together with your colleagues from Talent Management, to identify the candidates for the next round and starting the selection process. The good news, once entering year two of the ExCom Sponsorship Program, the ExCom members will have seen its value. Very often they cite, how much they benefited themselves from the program. Incorporate the feedback and off you are for round two. To see long lasting change and improvement in female representation at the senior level, we recommend running the program at least for five consecutive years. A number of organizations have applied the 'waterfall approach', by cascading the program further within the organization at a regional or functional level. This is particularly impactful, as you can dig deeper into the female talent pipeline, or lack thereof.

A good practice is starting the next program by combining the kick-off-event with both the outgoing and incoming cohort of senior female leaders in the same room with the ExCom. We have seen, how powerful the energy in the room is, when you have twice the number of ExCom members representing high potential senior women. A wonderful and almost side effect is the comradery and sense of alumni amongst the women, past and present participants.

5. ONE YEAR

The ExCom Sponsorship Program runs for one year, 12 months. Overall, we recommend running the program for five consecutive years, to see lasting change and embed formal and informal Sponsorship in the DNA of the organization.

6. OTHER PROGRAMS – REVERSE MENTORING

While we believe that this program particularly lends itself to Gender Equality and getting more women to the top, we appreciate that similar approaches can be successful for Race & Ethnicity, LGBTQ+, Age Diversity and Disability. What particularly stands out is the so-called *Reverse Mentoring*, where the focus is less on Exposure and more for the ExCom to get a sound understanding of underrepresented groups within the organization.

QUICK SUMMARY: EXECUTIVE SPONSORSHIP PROGRAM

- The Executive Sponsorship Program is a powerful tool to foster the development of key female talent and yields year-over-year results
- The underlying concept for career progression is the PIE (Performance, Image, Exposure) model. As career decisions are human decision, who knows you (i.e., Exposure) makes a big difference
- This program is highly practical and can be applied throughout your organization.

XXIV. SUPPLIER DIVERSITY

There are many aspects of D&I that come quite naturally to us when we try to think about the concepts or about solutions, but this one is being left out more often than you might think, yet the impact it can make has tremendous potential. Ideally, you want your supplier base to be a reflection of your employees and your customers.

But what is supplier diversity?

If we imagine that your organization is a person, it co-exists within a social network together with other human beings. And it absolutely matters who do we hang out with, how diverse is our network of personal. Following the same analogy, have you asked yourself, who is your organization hanging out with? Like an individual, an organization in today's world does not exist in an isolated silo bubble. No matter how small or big you are, you can't run a company without partnering with various suppliers, providers, co-collaborators, someone to do your accounting, someone to run your trainings, someone to process your payslips, someone to source your coffee, etc... All of these partners represent the "who is your organization hanging out with". And as we get to choose who do we hire; we also get to choose who do we work with on a B2B level.

The goal of supplier diversity is to create a level playing field in the marketplace, so that all businesses have an equal chance to compete for contracts, regardless of the owner's background. In recent years, there has been an increase in the number of companies that have committed to supplier diversity. This is largely due to the growing movement for social and racial justice, as well as the realization that supplier diversity can be beneficial for companies. There are numerous benefits of supplier diversity, including increased competition, higher quality products and services, and the ability to tap into new markets. In addition, supplier diversity can help to create a more sustainable and ethical supply chain. According to the Hackett Group, "companies that allocate 20 % or more of their spend to diverse suppliers attribute 10-15 % of their annual sales to supplier diversity programs. Conversely, companies that direct less than 20% of spend to diverse suppliers' attribute under 5 % of sales to their supplier diversity program."

In a way, it is a powerful strategy that attacks at the root, goes to the initial stages of sourcing and it brings systematic changes. It is a practice of your organization and specifically your procurement team that creates an inclusive economy that every business can benefit from.

Traditionally, supply chains and procurements were a cost-effectiveness strategy. Let's have a few big partners, they deliver a good service and most importantly the cost goes down as you can negotiate great deals. In fact, why place eight different orders from eight different suppliers when you can just work with two suppliers, place two bulk orders and you are done. And indeed, let's say it worked so far. Until Covid happened and these strategies were crushed in front of our faces. Businesses depended on one or two big partners, and when these partners had a crisis or had to close down or pause production, voilà. We realized that fewer suppliers lead to more dependency and more risk during times of crisis. As we can see, these strategies have only a short term and economic goal.

Now, how can we create equity in the business community?

- Your procurement department and strategy have to move away from transactional and cost effective only focus;
- Diverse and equitable considerations need to be introduced as part of the supplier selection criteria;
- Set a numerical goal to partner with the different categories of the supplier diverse partners*: women-owned, LGBTQ+ owned, minority-owned, disability-owned, small businesses, etc... (these are the most common categories;
- Hold your suppliers accountable to respect your D&I practices and demand that they have their own as well;
- Collaborate with local suppliers instead of opting out for global providers, the local organizations know the market better and already serve your communities;

- You are not alone - partner with every business leader who is a procurement customer, partner with your D&I team and make your strategy visible to the organization. Much like the overall topic of D&I, the procurement team is only the catalyst of this show. It takes a change of mindset and habits of the actual leaders in your organization to think differently when considering choosing a new provider for their need.

Making a commitment to supplier diversity can help your business tap into new markets, deepen your relationships with the communities you serve, and promote economic growth.

*The business to be at least 51 percent owned and operated by a member of a diverse or marginalized community

QUICK SUMMARY: SUPPLIER DIVERSITY

- Supplier diversity refers to the use of minority-owned businesses as suppliers, and a supplier diversity program is a proactive business program which encourages such use within an organization's supply chain. A diverse supplier is a business that is at least 51% owned and operated by an individual or group that is part of a traditionally underrepresented or underserved group
- Increasing your supplier diversity adds more supplier options to your supply chain. More supplier choices mean greater competition and better pricing, product quality, and service levels. Working with a broader range of supplier backgrounds leads to more innovation in products, services, and solutions
- Corporations like yours spend 58 cents of every dollar in revenue on payments to suppliers and can therefore benefit by increasing their diversity, as well as demonstrating their commitment to corporate social responsibility.

XXV. MARKETING, INNOVATION AND EMPLOYER BRANDING

In recent years, there's been a significant societal push for more diversity in the workplace. But did you know that more diverse teams are actually smarter and more creative?

Diverse teams are more creative because a person's individual creativity is enhanced by their ability to integrate different viewpoints, something many of us learn by interacting with people from different walks of life. Diversity is how you think, how you create knowledge, how you learn, and how you can look at a problem from a completely different perspective. Scientists believe that diverse teams can outperform homogeneous teams in decision making because they process information more carefully. More variety can also change how entire teams absorb the information they need to make better decisions.

Research shows us that in addition to saving a company from bad decisions, diverse teams can significantly increase innovation and profits. Team members with different backgrounds come up with different solutions, leading to more informed decision making and better outcomes. This is because diverse teams are especially good at debunking and correcting erroneous thoughts, generating more and more new ideas, and taking into account a wider range of variables when planning.

The concept behind what we call "diverse teams = better teams" can partially be explained by the idea of cognitive elaboration in the Elaboration Likelihood Model – the process of comprehending information by thinking critically, active learning, active listening, developing schemas and expanding our knowledge. As we see in diverse teams, the same cognitive elaboration technique comes much more naturally to people from underrepresented groups. Or should we say, to people who have faced systemic discrimination and inequalities for prolonged periods of time.

For example, when a woman is preparing to go to an interview, matching the job requirements is just not good enough. She has to take into consideration if she needs makeup or not, is her hair brushed or appears too messy, is her outfit professional enough or too revealing, triple check that she meets 100% of the job criteria, if she is nice, polite and smiling will this be mistaken for flirting, are there people like her in senior positions, are there enough restrooms for women in the office etc. A huge list of additional factors she is now used to considering that influence her decision, fact checking and critically choosing her new workplace. What it comes down to, is that she is making a thoroughly informed decision based on many variables. This, is what team members from underrepresented groups bring to the table of radical innovation.

So, easy right? So, we just need to take several people from different backgrounds, put them in a room, give them a challenge to work on and boom – the mind-blowing innovation is here. Not so fast :). Don't forget the second two letters of D&I. This is when the environment you create comes into play. Do these diverse people feel valued, listened to, with equitable opportunities for growth and a space of belonging? If they do, you've done a great job. If they don't, you can easily kiss goodbye the promises of diverse = better, as they will simply leave. Or imagine even worse - they stay, and you created the perfect recipe for unengaged workforce starting the journey of "quiet quitting".

Innovations are revolutionary ideas that people can create by teaming up in diverse and inclusive teams. At this point, it should easily come to your mind that diverse, inclusive and equitable teams are like idea factories —they are literally made to innovate and create a better.

On top of diverse teams being able to better implement radical innovations, they also anticipate changes in consumer needs and consumption patterns much faster. Yes, at this point of the chapter, we are going to explore even more directly the link of D&I to marketing, profitability and the employer brand image, and you will understand why it is an unavoidable part of the D&I puzzle.

While increasing revenue shouldn't be the only reason to consider diversity, equity, and inclusion (D&I) in your marketing, it certainly shows that consumers are willing to invest in brands that value them. By reaching to a wider population, greater diversity and inclusiveness contribute to a more coherent society. The benefits of diversity and inclusiveness can be seen in recruitment and retention, and customer acquisition and retention. Some business leaders understand the well-documented benefits that having a diverse workforce can bring to their company's culture and the employer brand image they cast to the world. Because let's not kid ourselves, at the moment, we live in a world of capitalism and consumerism, so if we take that corporations are existing as default, the smart thing to do is leverage their presence to advance our society at large.

The employer brand is your company's value proposition and reputation that current and prospective employees use to evaluate whether or not your company is an attractive place to work. D&I is key to seeing and understanding how an organization is perceived by employees, business partners, candidates, respondents, and other stakeholders, which at some point have a significant impact on an employer's branding strategy. With D&I at the forefront of both companies and the minds of job seekers, it's imperative that your employer brand includes the talent you hope to attract.

According to Glassdoor's 2020 Surveys, 76% of job seekers and employees say a diverse workforce is an important factor when evaluating companies and jobs. In a study by PwC (2015), 86% of female and 74% of male millennials consider a company's D&I policy when deciding their employer of choice.

Build a diversified business and a value chain in which underrepresented groups are empowered and don't be scared to make them visible as role models for change. Just recently, the first trailer for the movie version of the ultra-famous Disney cartoon The Little Mermaid was presented to the world. This wonderful fantasy tale, that describes the life of a mermaid, a creature that is in fact, not real and a character, that is not real. Within just a few hours of the trailer being uploaded on Youtube, there were 2 million dislikes on the video, all because the actress chosen to portray Ariel, this imaginary character, is black. On the other side of this, you could see parents showing the trailer to their kids for the first time and recording their reactions, shocked with disbelief and excitement, "whaaat, mommy, whaat? She is like me? I can be a princess as well?? You have got to be kidding me", etc.

What we see here is the ultimate exemplification of "representation matters". Inclusive employer brand offers multiple reflections on who your customer is and, when done effectively, inspires all members of your audience to feel like your brand understands them. At the heart of unlocking these opportunities is a simple yet powerful concept that will also change the way the world is evolving.

Failure to integrate D&I into your employer brand can create disasters. Failure to integrate D&I into your brand can give the impression that diversity is not a priority for your company and that you don't believe in the greater cause of D&I and that ultimately, you don't care about your people. If in the example above we witness that Disney did well in this particular instance of portraying an inclusive brand, there is a different more dangerous side to doing quite the opposite.

It was in September 2013, when the CEO of Barilla, the pasta giant, was driving his car on a way to a meeting with his chairman, Guido Barilla. Instead of listening to some music, he turned on the radio, as he knew Guido will give an interview to the national Italian station Radio 24. And then he hears the following sentence: "I would never make a commercial with a homosexual family. Not out of a lack of respect but because I do not see it like they do. My idea of family is a classic family where the woman has a fundamental role." Well, you can imagine what happened after. The hashtag boicotta-barilla was trending on Twitter, Harvard and other institutions removed the brand from their menus, celebrities boycotted the brand publicly, and within one year, the brand reputation dropped by 21%.

For job seekers today, having the right job position and a good salary is not good enough anymore. There is an even heavier emphasis on what they call an emotional salary, which constitutes of growth opportunities, belonging, D&I commitment, social responsibility, wellbeing, freedom, trust and accountability.

For consumers today, having just a commodity, a product or a service that just has the features they promise is not good enough anymore. People need to feel seen, will hold you responsible, need to see the story and the connection with your brand on a deeper level that is aligned with the values they live in, or they go somewhere else.

For the world today, existing as an organization and an employer who pays their taxes and makes the economy moving is not good enough anymore. Governments, NGOs, international organizations need from corporations to step their level up and show up to advance the equity in our society.

And we hope in the next edition of this book we will have the following sentence included, as today it is far from reality:

For all the CEOs today, they won't stay silent to their shareholders and won't accept the job of leading a company unless D&I is at the core of what they do.

QUICK SUMMARY: MARKETING & INNOVATION AND EMPLOYER BRANDING

- A bad or false reputation is difficult to recover from and can cost millions in hiring and re-branding expense
- Failure to integrate Diversity, Equity, and Inclusion as part of your employer brand can paint the picture that D&I isn't a priority to your company and its leadership
- Authenticity is key to any D&I initiative. When it comes to D&I, words have to be backed up by genuine action and accountability.

XXVI. ORGANIZATIONAL NETWORK ANALYSIS

We are 100% certain that you have been asked to measure inclusion in your organization more times that you can count, and we have been through the same struggle. But how to do it? Just asking your employees "Hi Becky, do you feel included today?" - is just not going to cut it anymore.

In every organization there is your typical and very visible org chart, who reports to who and who works in which team. And, on the other hand there is the invisible, practical org chart – the networks of relationships that your employees use to solve problems, get work done, make decisions, and ultimately get that nice promotion in the pocket. We need to be aware of the fact that the networks we create are not just a reflection of our skills and our interests, but also of the social norms and biases in which we have been raised. So, in the sense of visible versus invisible networks, who doesn't love a good reveal? These networks can be unveiled via a methodology called Organizational Network Analysis, or simply ONA. Think of it as an x-ray scan of your organization. Whether you're a business leader, a consultant, or an academic, the chances are not big that you've heard of Organizational Network Analysis, but not to worry, you are in good hands, and we are on a world mission to change that. What exactly does ONA entail and how can it be used to gain insight into an organization's structure, performance, and culture? As part of The Inclusion Foundation™, we have taken the best bits of ONA and below, we will provide an overview of its methodology and potential applications.

Organizational Network Analysis (ONA) is a methodology that has emerged in recent years as a way to explore the intricate networks of social relationships and behaviors within organizations. Essentially, ONA can help us understand how people interact with each other – something that could benefit any organization in terms of strategy, communication and efficiency. Your organization can use this knowledge to your advantage, creating a better working environment for the employees and a more inclusive workplace overall. With ONA, it's easier for people, teams and organizations to better understand the complexities of how their various collaborators interact with one another. It is an exciting new field which promises to revolutionize the world of how we perceive organizations and even more, inclusion within them.

How does it work?

ONA introduced a new approach which combines analytical techniques from network science, system dynamics, and strategy design - offering an all-inclusive view of how different systems can interact. In simpler words, we know that the root cause of exclusion and discrimination lies in the systems and structures that surrounds us. Once you will see the results, you can learn to structure their networks in more efficient ways, and gain insight into how their systems are interconnected. This knowledge is invaluable and makes working with these complex networks easier on all levels, leading to improved inclusion overall.

The process begins with data collection - a web and mobile friendly survey consisting of only 7 questions gathers some details from your employees. These questions cover several dimensions which are of crucial importance to showcase and quantify the complexities of Diversity & Inclusion in the workplace. The questions have been specifically designed to be structured and simplistic so as to maximise the efficacy of their analysis. In addition to the 7 simplistic questions below, participants will be asked to self-identify their gender, age, sexual orientation and race & ethnicity. The explored dimensions are flexible depending on the organization's needs.

1. Who do you turn to for fast results?
2. Who do you involve first when given a challenging task?
3. When you want to challenge a corporate decision, to whom do you first turn for guidance?
4. Imagine you finished a project, presentation or task, who in your team do you turn to for honest feedback?
5. When you hear the word 'change agent', who comes to your mind?
6. When a new employee arrives, who would you recommend talking to when it comes to the question 'how are things done around here'?
7. You are about to receive some difficult company news, who do you prefer to hear it from first?

Once the data is collected, our AI algorithms will process and analyze the data, to be finally displayed in a visual representation of all the nodes of the different networks. This is powerful toolkit to meaningfully analyze complex organizations. The results don't look at the data top-down but have the individual in the center. It can help us access data and insights that would otherwise remain hidden, allowing us to uncover the true nature of an organization's dynamics and make more informed decisions.

What do the results look like? One way that organizational network analytics (ONA) can be used to measure inclusion is by looking at the patterns of communication and collaboration within the organization. If a group of employees consistently communicates and works on projects together but does not include individuals from diverse backgrounds or departments, this may indicate a lack of inclusion. For example, we were examining the relationships with the ONA tool at a client whose workforce split was 80% men and 20% women. While investigating the dimensions of who the employees turn to when they need fast results, 30% of the employees mentioned were women and 70% were men. This might seem like good news, as even if women represent 20% of the population, still they represented one third – 30% of all of the mentions in the survey. Nevertheless, once we looked deeper into the details of the patterns of communication, we found out that still, women were the ones mostly turning to other women for getting fast results and men were excluding women for these requests.

At this point, we are just scratching the surface of ONA here. It is a revolutionary educational tool that provides a new way of examining complex systems. This inclusion-oriented method promises to bridge the divide between traditional org charts and the invisible world, by delivering outcomes that are tailored to people's individual behavior and sense of belonging. The result is a powerful solution for understanding who interacts with whom, for what reasons, and how this may affect your business strategy in the future. Ultimately, with the power of AI, you will be able to understand how people are connected and do something about it.

QUICK SUMMARY: ORGANIZATIONAL NETWORK ANALYSIS

- Organizational network analysis (ONA) is a quantitative method for modeling and analyzing how communications, information, decisions, and resources flow through your organization
- When it comes to Inclusion, we also talk about "an X-ray of your organization". One of the bottlenecks of Diversity, Equity, and Inclusion initiatives is that there is very little data available to measure if inclusion is actually taking place. We recommend identifying and to analyze relationship networks across your entire organization to generate valuable insights regarding inclusion
- We trust in data as much as you do.

XXVII. TAKE AWAY

For fast readers like you, we've compiled all QUICK SUMMARIES here. They sum-up the key messages and takeaway in form of an abstract. Before reading on, try for yourself, what comes to mind for each chapter.

THE BROADER CONTEXT

THE EVOLUTION OF DIVERSITY, EQUITY & INCLUSION

- The D&I movement started in the 1960's and is not new
- D&I is ever evolving - a journey rather than a destination
- Today D&I mostly extends to: Gender Equality, LGBTQ+ Inclusion, NWOW, Wellbeing & Mental Health, Age Diversity, Socioeconomic Inclusion, Race & Ethnicity and Persons with Disabilities.

MYTHS & COMMON MISTAKES

- Diversity, Equity, and Inclusion is another HR initiative. D&I expands beyond HR and collaborates with numerous internal and external stakeholders. Anchoring D&I solely within HR might give an excuse to the rest of your organization not to get involved
- D&I is NOT a zero-sum game. The assumption that the inclusion of new people, especially in

leadership, leads to the exclusion or expulsion of those who are already there is categorically false. Having a diverse workforce means happier and healthier employees, customers feel more respected, and managers have greater access to the talent and skillset they need for their organizations to thrive

- Pink-washing, rainbow-washing and unconscious bias training don't work.

PSYCHOLOGICAL SAFETY

- Psychological Safety is a precursor to high-performing teams
- Belonging happens when people feel psychologically safe
- Psychological safety is the shared belief that a team is safe for interpersonal risk-taking.

QUICK SUMMARY: THE 'H' in AI

- The moment is now to act upon making sure that there is enough 'H' in AI
- There is a real danger of AI bias. AI bias is the underlying prejudice in data that's used to create AI algorithms, which can ultimately result in discrimination and other social consequences
- Another reason why AI might be discriminatory is quite obvious: The lack of diversity in the sector.

NWOW - THE FUTURE OF WORK

- The future of work describes changes in how work will get done over the next decade, influenced by technological, generational, and societal shifts
- Work will increasingly be a fluid-concept and the standard 9-to-5 working week will be rare, while the divisions between home and work further blur and non-financial rewards are given in trade-off for less money
- The inclusive workplace in high demand: Organizations' shift their attention to racial injustice and equity, including real commitments and investments in doing better.

#METOO, WOKE, CANCEL CULTURE & CULTURAL APPROPRIATION

- What started with #Metoo, led to the birth of cancel culture, wokeness and cultural appropriation
- These can have a chilling effect on public discourse, might be unproductive, don't bring real social change, can cause intolerance and amount to cyberbullying
- Might be hampering your Diversity, Equity, and Inclusion plans.

THE "S" IN ESG

- The "S" in ESG or: How to invest in your people

- The social component of ESG covers all the ways companies interact with their employees and communities in which they operate
- How corporations measure their social impact can greatly influence how they address the wellbeing of their employees, communities, and other stakeholders.

THE INCLUSION FOUNDATION ™

- An independent, third party verified company based in Switzerland that certifies organizations around the world in Diversity, Equity, and Inclusion
- The assessment spans over seven key dimensions of D&I: Gender Balance, LGBTQ+ Inclusion, Race & Ethnicity, Persons with Disabilities, Wellbeing & Mental Health, NWOW the future of work and Age Diversity
- A smart approach using AI to measure Inclusion (ONA) is embedded.

INTERSECTIONALITY

- The concept of intersectionality describes the ways in which systems of inequality based on gender, race, ethnicity, sexual orientation, gender identity, disability, class, and other forms of discrimination "intersect" to create unique dynamics and compounding effects
- All forms of inequality are mutually reinforcing and must therefore be analyzed and addressed

simultaneously to prevent one form of inequality from reinforcing another

- Professor Kimberle Crenshaw coined the term in 1989 as a way to help explain the oppression of African American women.

ORGANIZATION

OPERATING MODEL

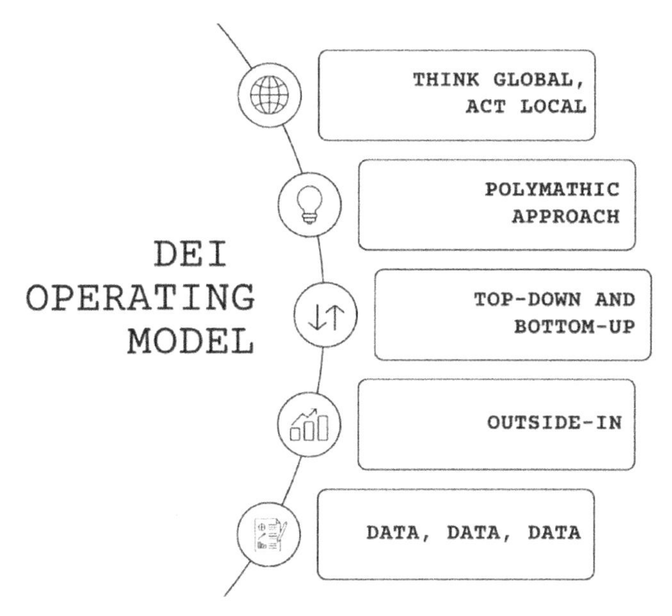

GENDER BALANCE

- Gender Equality was made part of international human rights law by the Universal Declaration of

Human Rights, which was adopted by the UN General Assembly on 10 December 1948

- Achieving full gender equality, one of the 17 Sustainable Development Goals (SDGs) could take close to 300 years if the current rate of progress continues according to the United Nations
- Organizations play a significant role by setting clear gender goals, attracting and retaining female talent, fostering career development via Executive Sponsorship, actively involving men in driving progress, ensuring Equal Pay and implementing an inclusive Family Leave policy.

LGBTQ+ INCLUSION

- LGBTQ+ is an abbreviation for lesbian, gay, bisexual, transgender, queer, or questioning
- Rights affecting lesbian, gay, bisexual, transgender and queer people vary greatly by country or jurisdiction - encompassing everything from the legal recognition of same-sex marriage to the death penalty for homosexuality
- Organizations can help advance LGBTQ+ Inclusion around the world by applying the "Embassy" model, where they create an inclusive workplace internally for their LGBTQ+ colleagues without seeking to change laws or societal attitudes
- T stands for Transgender, not Too difficult to deal with.

AGE DIVERSITY

- The age diversity definition is simply "the acceptance of employees of different ages in the workplace". Age-based diversity is similar to generational diversity in that it seeks to combat age discrimination
- There are four main generations who are currently active in today's workforce: Baby Boomers, Generation X, Millennials (e.g., Generation Y) and Generation Z
- Employers must understand that each of these generations has different strengths, preferences, and work styles that are determined by the world in which they grew up, their life stage, and their professional experience.

WELLBEING & MENTAL HEALTH

- The World Health Organization (WHO) describes mental health as a 'state of wellbeing in which every individual realizes their own potential, can cope with the normal stresses of life, and can work productively and fruitfully
- The COVID-19 pandemic has shown why employers must prioritize Wellbeing & Mental Health
- Companies are investing into Wellbeing & Mental Health to increase productivity and improved work performance, reduced absenteeism, turnover and injuries, and enhanced reputation increasing

recruitment and retention. Improved Mental Health also benefits overall Health.

SOCIO-ECONOMIC INCLUSION

- The socioeconomic status is a characterization derived from a "combination of education, income and occupation", and can seriously impact wellbeing and career opportunities
- Creating a socially diverse workforce is about removing barriers of entry ("class ceiling") and creating social mobility
- In place of four-year-degrees, many organizations are instead focusing on skills-based hiring to widen the talent pool.

RACE & ETHNICITY

- Race and ethnicity are not the same. Race is a social construct that has historically been used to classify human beings according to physical or biological characteristics. Ethnicity is something a person acquires or ascribes to and refers to as shared culture, such as language, practices, and beliefs
- The complexities are vast and very much depend on where your organization operates
- Europe is increasingly marked by cultural diversity and foreign-born populations. In addition, being black in the EU often means racism and poor jobs, as black people in the EU face unacceptable

difficulties in getting a decent job because of their skin color.

PEOPLE WITH DISABILITIES

- Person's disabilities include those who have long-term physical, mental, intellectual, or sensory impairments which, in interaction with various barriers, may hinder their full and effective participation in the workplace
- People with disabilities make up an estimated one billion, or 15 %, of the world's population. About 80 % are of working age. The right of people with disabilities to decent work, however, is frequently denied. People with disabilities, particularly women with disabilities, face enormous attitudinal, physical, and informational barriers to equal opportunities in the world of work.
- To be successful in sourcing and acquiring talent with disabilities, it is important to successfully prepare your recruiters and future employees. Measures employers are implementing range from (physical) accessibility to active inclusion within the team.

CEO LEADERSHIP

- Diversity, Equity, and Inclusion have taken a center stage on many corporate agendas. This has largely been driven by increased social justice pressure from investors, boards, media and society. It is important to remember that diversifying the workforce is not only the right thing to do, but it also makes good business sense

- In this book, supported by ample research, we have shown that focusing on D&I, leads to increased innovation, better business outcomes and increased workplace effectiveness
- Increasingly, CEOs are implementing their D&I strategy like any other business strategy. The same internal tracking mechanism is applied. It is equally important to communicate openly and authentically about progress vs goals internally and externally.

EMPLOYEE RESOURCE GROUPS (ERGs)

- Why are they called 'Resource Groups'? ERGs have historically been diversity and inclusion networks that allowed professionals to connect. ERGs, originally called workplace affinity groups, began in the 1960s in response to racial tensions in the United States. Nowadays, ERGs are powerful resources for facilitating discussions and providing networks for professionals based on shared identities, experiences and allyship.
- In the past few decades, companies have expanded ERG topics and begun implementing chapters worldwide, and today, ERGs are integrated into business strategies as imperatives. Top ranked companies have ERGs.

- Wherever D&I sits within your organization, we recommend an independent ERG budget sitting within your Corporate Strategy department or similar.

KEY STAKEHOLDERS

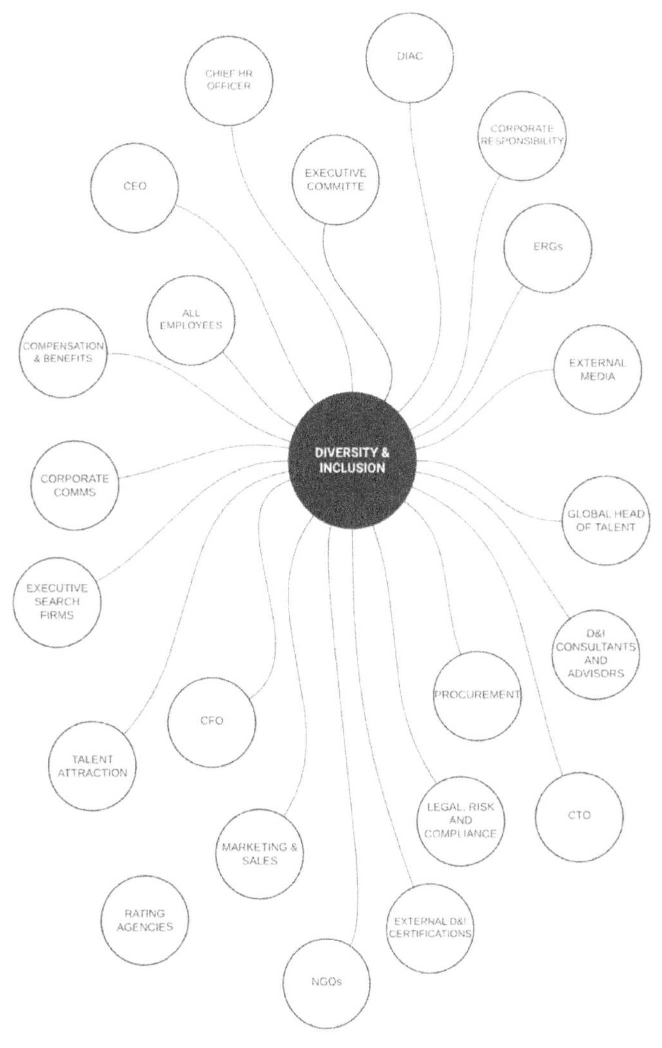

AVOIDING BACKLASH:

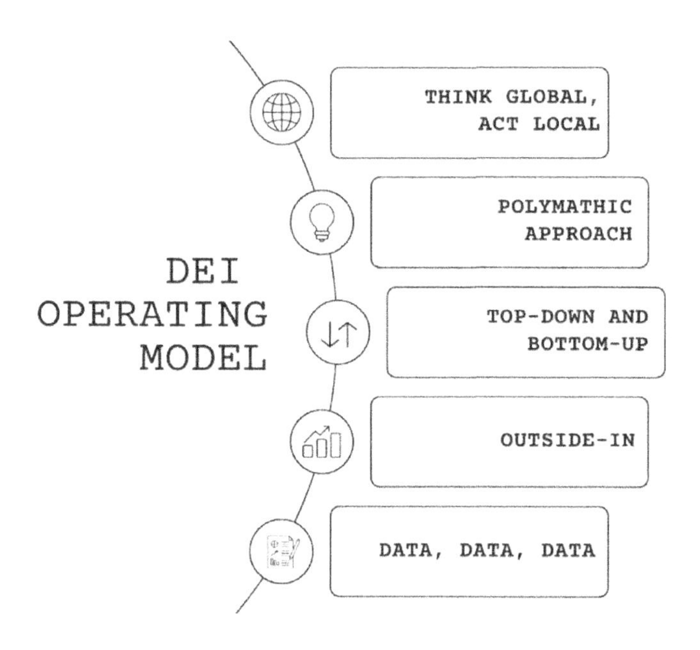

RECOURCES

INCLUSIVE LEAVES

- Nowadays, there are a number of Inclusive Leaves to consider: Family Leave, Sabbatical Leave, Bereavement Leave, Leave for Volunteering, Leave for Menstruation and Menopause, Disability Leave and Gender Transition Leave
- Traditionally, menopause and menstrual leave have been taboo topics. More recently though, an ever-increasing number of organizations have

implemented both menopause and menstrual leave to eliminate the taboo and to recognize the physical and mental discomforts they can cause.

- Enacting inclusive paid leave policies benefit both the employer and employee, as they help to attract and retain top talent. Prospective employees value workplaces that demonstrate a commitment to the health and wellbeing of all employees and their diverse families.

EXECUTIVE SPONSORSHIP PROGRAM

- The Executive Sponsorship Program is a powerful tool to foster the development of key female talent and yields year-over-year results
- The underlying concept for career progression is the PIE (Performance, Image, Exposure) model. As career decisions are human decision, who knows you (i.e., Exposure), makes a big difference
- This program is highly practical and can be applied throughout your organization.

SUPPLIER DIVERSITY

- Supplier diversity refers to the use of minority-owned businesses as suppliers, and a supplier diversity program is a proactive business program which encourages such use within an organization's supply chain. A diverse supplier is a business that is at least 51% owned and operated by an individual or group that is part of a traditionally underrepresented or underserved group

- Increasing your supplier diversity adds more supplier options to your supply chain. More supplier choices mean greater competition and better pricing, product quality, and service levels. Working with a broader range of supplier backgrounds leads to more innovation in products, services, and solutions
- Corporations like yours spend 58 cents of every dollar in revenue on payments to suppliers and can therefore benefit by increasing their diversity, as well as demonstrating their commitment to corporate social responsibility.

ORGANIZATIONAL NETWORK ANALYSIS

- Organizational Network Analysis (ONA) is a quantitative method for modeling and analyzing how communications, information, decisions, and resources flow through your organization
- When it comes to Inclusion, we also talk about "an X-ray of your organization". One of the bottlenecks of Diversity, Equity, and Inclusion initiatives is that there is very little data available to measure if inclusion is actually taking place. We recommend identifying and analyzing relationship networks across your entire organization to generate valuable insights regarding inclusion
- We trust in data as much as you do.

MARKETING & INNOVATION AND EMPLOYER BRANDING

- A bad or false reputation is difficult to recover from and can cost millions in hiring and re-branding expense
- Failure to integrate Diversity, Equity, and Inclusion as part of your employer brand can paint the picture that D&I isn't a priority to your company and its leadership
- Authenticity is key to any D&I initiative. When it comes to D&I, words have to be backed up by genuine action and accountability.

XXVIII. AFTERWORD

As we are coming to the end, we would like to celebrate the serendipity that brought us together and made this book possible. Surely, all of you know this feeling of: "Imagine, what if I wouldn't have been there on this exact date? How different would my life have turned out to be?"

We wrote this book the way we preach: Asynchronous. We weren't once in the same room during the writing process. But, one day back in March 2019, we were! And now, we will hear individually and independently, how this went down.

To Christiane:

In the halls of IMD, a friendship that started in chance,
two strangers at a conference, friendship bigger than
romance.
Hesitant to make small talk with new friends, I found
myself with a tall blond and conversations with no ends.

Confident and bold, with a voice that mirrored my own, I
found someone who got me inside and out, and I knew our
friendship was what life was all about.

As we talked it felt like I found a kindred soul.
The diva in my head, now personified and whole.
We laughed and debated, shared our dreams and goals,
discussed diversity, white privilege, and cannabis rolls.

I poured my heart, my dream to fight inequality, she
understood my vision and gave me a sense of clarity.

Now, with all my heart, I say thank you for being the
friend that feels so true.
To all the memories we will make, and to all the dreams
we will together undertake.

For Aleks:

A glass of red wine in my hand, standing at one of the high tables just outside of the IMD plenary room, surrounded by colleagues and strangers, I met Aleks for the first time.

His youthful confidence immediately stood out, radiating an energy that captivated me from the start. Firmly rooted in his flamboyant intelligence and wit, he said all the right things, with a smile larger-than-life.

As the night went on, our conversations grew bolder, our jokes juicier, and our laughter louder. With reactions of the speed of light and always a touch of caring.

This is when I knew that he was unique and challenging in all the ways I need.

Since that fateful day in March, we haven't left each other's side, fighting relentlessly for more equality in this world. He has been my rock and my inspiration. To be continued.

XXIX. ACKNOWLEDGEMENTS

We want to thank:

Donato, Kara, Kian, Kersten, Hendrik, Oliver, Udo, Ilse, Mark, Mathy, Svetlana, Dragi, Lihnida, Perrine, Cedric, Jana, Lara.

XXX. LITERATURE

Cox, T. H., Jr., & Blake, S. (1991). Managing cultural diversity: Implications for organizational competitiveness. Academy of Management Perspectives, 5(3), 45-56.

Page, S. E. (2007). The Difference: How the power of diversity creates better groups, firms, schools, and societies. Princeton University Press.

Williams, K. Y., & O'Reilly, C. A., III. (1998). Demography and diversity in organizations: A review of 40 years of research. Research in Organizational Behavior, 20, 77-140.

Bell, M. P., & Harrison, D. A. (1996). Using intra-national diversity for international assignments: A model of bicultural competence and expatriate adjustment. Academy of Management Journal, 39(2), 525-549.

Herring, C. (2009). Does diversity pay?: Race, gender, and the business case for diversity. American Sociological Review, 74(2), 208-224.

Kalev, A., Dobbin, F., & Kelly, E. (2006). Best practices or best guesses? Assessing the efficacy of corporate affirmative action and diversity policies. American Sociological Review, 71(4), 589-617.

Richard, O. C., & Johnson, N. B. (2001). Understanding the impact of human resource diversity practices on firm performance. Journal of Managerial Issues, 13(2), 177-195.

Nishii, L. H. (2013). The benefits of diversity in organizations: Implications for the workplace, human resource development, and career development. European Journal of Training and Development, 37(1), 1-12.

Jackson, S. E., Joshi, A., & Erhardt, N. L. (2003). Recent research on team and organizational diversity: SWOT analysis and implications. Journal of Management, 29(6), 801-830.

Edmondson, A. C. (1999). Psychological safety and learning behavior in work teams. Administrative Science Quarterly, 44(2), 350-383.

Edmondson, A. C. (2014). Building a psychologically safe workplace. Harvard Business Review, 92(1/2), 104-111.

Kahn, W. A. (1990). Psychological conditions of personal engagement and disengagement at work. Academy of Management Journal, 33(4), 692-724.

Butler, J. (1990). Gender Trouble: Feminism and the Subversion of Identity. Routledge.

Halberstam, J. (2011). The Queer Art of Failure. Duke University Press.

Sedgwick, E. K. (1990). Epistemology of the Closet. University of California Press.

Eagly, A. H., & Karau, S. J. (2002). Role congruity theory of prejudice toward female leaders. Psychological Review, 109(3), 573-598.

World Economic Forum. (2021). The Global Gender Gap Report 2021. Retrieved from https://www.weforum.org/reports/gender-gap-2021-report-100-years-pay-equality

Bagues, M., & Esteve-Volart, B. (2010). Can Gender Parity Break the Glass Ceiling? Evidence from a Repeated Randomized Experiment. Review of Economic Studies, 77(4), 1301-1328.

OECD. (2019). The Pursuit of Gender Equality: An Uphill Battle. Retrieved from https://www.oecd.org/gender/the-pursuit-of-gender-equality-9789264281318-en.htm

Ng, T. W. H., & Feldman, D. C. (2010). The relationship of age to ten dimensions of job performance. Journal of Applied Psychology, 95(5), 944-960.

Kunze, F., Boehm, S. A., & Bruch, H. (2013). Age diversity, age discrimination climate, and performance consequences—a cross organizational study. Journal of Organizational Behavior, 34(6), 881-902.

Shipton, H., Budhwar, P. S., Sparrow, P., & Brown, A. (2016). HRM and innovation: Looking across levels. Journal of Management Studies, 53(4), 610-632.

Bezrukova, Katerina,Spell, Chester S.,Perry, Jamie L.,Jehn, Karen A. Psychological Bulletin, Vol 142(11), Nov 2016, 1227-1274. A meta-analytical integration of over 40 years of research on diversity training evaluation.

J Pers Soc Psychol. 2013 Aug;105(2):171-92. Predicting ethnic and racial discrimination: a meta-analysis of IAT criterion studies.

XXXI. ABOUT THE AUTHORS

Christiane Bisanzio

Christiane Bisanzio is more than just a lawyer. She's a forward-thinking pioneer in the sphere of Diversity, Equity, and Inclusion (DEI), having led organizational development, talent management, and DEI strategies with poise and vision.

Her contributions to the field have been widely recognized, with The Economist acknowledging her as one of the global Top 50 D&I Leaders as early as 2013. This accolade has been reinforced by multiple nominations in the years since, including her 2022 recognition as one of the most influential DEI Leaders in EMEA. This acknowledgement underscores her ongoing commitment to making a significant impact in her industry. In addition to her DEI advocacy, Christiane also applies her strategic acumen in Non-Executive Director (NED) roles. Her innovative thinking and exceptional problem-solving skills have enabled her to lead teams through complex projects with notable success. Christiane's expertise extends beyond DEI. She's a respected thought leader and public speaker on matters related to People & Culture, using her platform to shape industry dialogue and influence perspectives.

At the crossroads of innovation and progressive leadership, Christiane Bisanzio stands as a beacon in today's ever-evolving corporate world. Away from her professional commitments, Christiane cherishes her personal life in Geneva, Switzerland. There, she shares her home with her Italian husband, their two teenage children, and a beloved family dog.

Aleksandar Damchevski

Aleksandar (he/she/they) is an internationally acclaimed author, economist, technologist, transfeminist and HR strategist.

Armed with a background in economics, medicine and computer science, Aleksandar embodies a bold, inclusive vision. As the co-founder of two organizations focused on creating an inclusive future, he is shifting the paradigms of inclusion across Europe. His expertise, honed over 15 years of leadership in multinational corporations, manifests in ground-breaking strategies that center the human value within institutional structures.

With a personal journey as an immigrant, she understands the priceless value of human relationships, with an ability to demystify complex concepts and attach meaning to our lives. She translates this understanding into captivating performances, making her a sought-after speaker and jury. As a judge at the prestigious Swiss Diversity Award, they highlight and celebrate innovation in the field of diversity. Their transdisciplinary perspective, marking the intersection of art, philosophy, queer theory and technology, enables them to skillfully navigate society and inspire lasting change.

Aleksandar Damchevski is more than a leader—they are an instigator of change, a passionate advocate for belonging and a bold visionary who constantly pushes boundaries to create a kinder future.

Printed in Great Britain
by Amazon